THE RUSTY RAKE GARDENER

Beautiful Canadian Gardens
with Minimum Toil

Dave and Cathy Cummins

with John Lawrence Reynolds

Macmillan Canada
Toronto

Canadian Cataloguing in Publication Data

Cummins, Dave
  The rusty rake gardener

Includes index.
ISBN 0–7715–7617–X

1. Low maintenance gardening – Canada. 2. Gardening – Canada.
I. Cummins, Cathy. II. Reynolds, John Lawrence. III. Title.

SB453.3.C2C85 1999   635.9'0971   C99–930284–1

This book is available at special discounts for bulk purchases by your group or organization for sales promotions, premiums, fundraising and seminars. For details, contact: Macmillan Canada, Special Sales Department, 29 Birch Avenue, Toronto, ON M4V 1E2. Tel: 416-963-8830.

Cover and interior design: Tania Craan
Cover photo: David Cummins
Back-cover photo of Cathy and David Cummins: John Lawrence Reynolds
Interior illustrations: Rob Cummins
Interior photos: pages 47, 81, 94, 104, 130, 137, John Lawrence Reynolds;
                   page 27 David and Cathy Cummins
Colour photos: John Lawrence Reynolds, David and Cathy Cummins
Composition: IBEX Graphic Communications Inc.

Macmillan Canada
Toronto, Ontario, Canada

1 2 3 4 5 TRI 03 02 01 00 99

Printed in Canada

To all the dedicated volunteer members of the
Royal Botanical Gardens Auxiliary

CONTENTS

Foreword   xi

Introduction   xiii

CHAPTER 1
Who's the Boss?   1

CHAPTER 2
When Do We Start Having Fun?   19

CHAPTER 3
Some Plants Have Time to Waste. Yours.   35

CHAPTER 4
The Roots of the Problem   50

CHAPTER 5
Tools, Tips and Tall Tales   72

CHAPTER 6
The Lawn as Simon Legree   84

CHAPTER 7
Rugged Individualists in Your Garden   99

CHAPTER 8
A Perennial List of Characters . . . and Vice Versa   120

CHAPTER 9
Annuals, Bulbs and Containers   135

CHAPTER 10
Thyme Is on Your Side   147

CHAPTER 11
The Joys of Starting from Scratch   159

CHAPTER 12
The More You Give, the More You Get   170

Index   175

ACKNOWLEDGEMENTS

Horticulture, like so many fields of endeavour, is a continuous learning experience. A number of people have influenced us over the years, and a great many more continue to add their support and share their knowledge.

In the early years, two Bills played major roles in helping us develop our passion for gardening. Unfortunately, both are no longer with us.

Bill Hartnell, a colourful radio personality known as "The Old Garden Doctor," sprinkled his expert advice with humour and folksy comments. He brought a spirit of fun and excitement to gardening for novices like us.

Bill Swanborough—Cathy's uncle—was both an avid gardener and eccentric character whose beautiful garden in Hamilton inspired us to start a garden of our own.

Jim Lounsbery, the owner of Vineland Nurseries and a popular horticultural lecturer, has been a friend for a number of years. His knowledge and enthusiasm have proved highly infectious to us.

We have benefitted in more ways than we can count from our involvement with the staff and associates of the Royal Botanical Gardens. We couldn't possibly name them all, but we want to mention three in particular:

Dr. Leslie Laking, former Director of the the RBG and now a fellow auxiliary member;

Chris Graham, Manager of Horticultural Services;

Dave Schmidt, Supervisor of Plant Propagation.

Credit must also go to our family for their continuing support in spite of our various behavioural disorders where plants are involved. Thanks to:

Joan and Bill Henwood, Dave's sister and brother-in-law;

Evelyn McNulty, Cathy's mother;

Carolyn and Fred Vanderlip, our daughter and son-in-law;

Our son, Rob Cummins, whose skill and training as a landscape designer has added so much to our garden's success, and whose talents as an illustrator can be found throughout this book.

Kathy Renwald has been supportive of our endeavours almost from the beginning, and has featured our garden on her HGTV show, "Gardener's Journal," on several occasions.

Finally, we are indebted to our long-time friend John Lawrence Reynolds, who has done a wonderful job moulding our words into a reader-friendly format.

FOREWORD

Dave and Cathy Cummins are the Merrill Lynch of horticulture. When they talk, people listen.

I know this first-hand. We have taped several segments of "Gardener's Journal" television program amid the flowers, shrubs and trees at their home in Dundas, Ontario. Back in 1993, Dave and Cathy were particularly smitten by the new 'Purple Wave' petunia. On camera, Dave showed off his prolific patch, which blanketed a corner of the garden with intense colour.

As soon as the episode was aired in the U.S. and Canada on HGTV (Home & Garden Television), we were deluged by a tidal wave of response. By phone, fax and e-mail, people all over North America sent desperate pleas, asking where they could obtain seeds for Purple Wave petunia.

The Cummins' have that effect on people. Blame it on their contagious enthusiasm (Dave's is gentle and technical, Cathy's is spirited and emotional) and their photogenic plants. That's an irresistible combination to gardeners.

Until *The Rusty Rake Gardener*, people were aware of the Cummins' gardening magic only through television appearances, Dave's presentations at the Royal Botanical Gardens and local gardening clubs as well as their annual Plantastic! spring sale.

For three days every May, the Cummins' yard is crammed with treasure hunters seeking new and unusual annuals, indestructible perennials, and the trees and shrubs that should be on everyone's Top Ten list—all raised and nurtured by Dave himself. Each plant is accompanied by a full-colour photo plus detailed instructions for planting and care. Dave mingles among the crowd, patiently answering questions and offering suggestions; Cathy leads tours of the spring garden and introduces everyone to their dog, Shamus.

This is no mere garden sale. It's a social event that "kicks off" the gardening season for many people in the Dundas area. One year, I bumped into a university professor who suggested that Dave and Cathy's plant sale could be a model for reviving a sense of community among our fortressed neighbourhoods. I think he has a point.

Their plant sale says much about Dave and Cathy's values. At a time when even horticulture risks becoming a competitive sport, Dave and Cathy prefer to share rather than show off. In their garden, everyone is at home—the novice feels welcome, and the expert feels inspired.

The Cummins' garden is always open to friends, and often to strangers. Dave and Cathy help raise money for charities by opening it to tours, and they can often be spotted volunteering at the Royal Botanical Gardens where they conduct tours, answer the "Hot Line," or pot plants for special sales.

Me, I'm selfish. I treasure the quiet moments in their garden, especially the mornings when Cathy hands me a cup of fresh coffee and I'm left to make the rounds by myself. There is time to admire the gingko tree, marvel at the berries on the porcelain vine, and wish the wisteria well over the winter.

With this book, many more people will be able to share the wisdom, experience and humour of this very special couple . . . and the extraordinary beauty of their garden.

—Kathy Renwald

PHOTO: TIM LEYES

Kathy Renwald is the host and producer of "Gardener's Journal," seen on HGTV and other TV outlets across North America and in Japan.

INTRODUCTION

Gardens are contradictory places. The best are private retreats, like the most personal rooms in a home. In this sense, a garden becomes a refuge, a place to withdraw from the world's problems, immerse yourself in natural beauty and leave the frenzy of modern life behind while you watch the day lilies nod in the sun and the butterflies visit the coneflowers.

But gardens should be public places as well. Where is the joy of surrounding yourself with lush, vibrant colour if no one arrives to admire your handwork? Well-planned and tended gardens are minor works of art, and art should be displayed for viewing and shared enjoyment.

We regard our garden as an extension of our home, so we welcome the arrival of visitors as an opportunity to share the beauty, express our creativity and—all right, we admit it—stroke our egos a little.

Often, a first-time visitor to our garden will turn to us and say, "Where do you find the time to care for this?" We're not surprised by the question, but the visitor is usually amazed by our answer. "It doesn't take nearly as much as you think," we reply. "And we enjoy practically every minute we spend in our garden, because we've found ways to minimize the chores and maximize the fun."

We're recently retired, which makes it easier to find the time than it is for some people. But while gardening to us is practically a year-round activity, even during our cold Canadian winters, it's far from our sole recreation.

We're not wedded to our garden; we're wedded to each other. Our life includes playing tennis (Dave) and performing in a vocal chorus (Cathy), plus spending time with active grandchildren, travelling abroad, volunteering for various duties at the nearby Royal Botanical Gardens, and maintaining a fairly busy social life.

Many visitors to our garden find this surprising. They assume that every plant we tend demands constant attention, just like small children. Well, we finished raising our children several years ago, and like all parents we learned (among other things) that it's unrealistic to expect only joy and beauty from your kids. There's going to be a little pain and stress along the way.

But your garden plants are not your children. You have a right to expect them to behave on their own and bring only joy and beauty into your life. Mind you, we love plants with a passion, and since Dave nurtures them from seedlings through to transplanting, he has a special soft spot for them.

Our philosophy is this: After a decent interval, for example two or three years, if plants continue refusing to obey and act so weird in public that they embarrass us, we yank 'em out and toss 'em on the compost heap. (No, you are not allowed to do this with your kids under similar circumstances.)

This philosophy has affected our entire approach to gardening, and we want to share that philosophy with you in this book. It is our view that the two words "garden" and "work" should never be used in the same sentence. "Puttering" is fine, but not "work" or "chores." When your garden is blooming virtually on its own and your rake is growing rusty from little use, you'll discover a broad smile on your face and more time on your hands.

So let's get started.

CHAPTER 1

WHO'S THE BOSS?

We understand how some people become sentimental about their plants. We're as guilty as anyone, but we try not to overdo it.

Every plant in your garden is directly related to the vegetables you ate for dinner and the wooden beams supporting the roof of your home. These plants exist to serve your needs, not vice versa. Remember this the next time your garden seems to be running your life.

Some people put up with behaviour and demands from their garden plants that they would never tolerate from their children, their dog, their cat or their in-laws. How long would you indulge a live-in brother-in-law who demanded a special diet, a weekly haircut and a private bed all because he just might, if he's in the right mood, look especially handsome three weeks of the year?

"If you loved him enough, you would do it," some might say.

We say turf him out. We have better things to do.

Over the years, we've worked out an agreement with the inhabitants of our garden; if they pull their weight, we'll make them comfortable. If they make too many demands, we'll turn them into compost. Sure, it's fun to tend the garden. But it's also fun to sit in the shade with a cold drink and admire our garden in full bloom, or curl up with a book in a shady corner while birds and butterflies flutter around us.

Many people spend too much time performing exhaustive chores and too little time enjoying their garden from a relaxed, maybe even a reclining, position. Attending to a garden is not the only reason to have one, after all. A garden is meant to be enjoyed, not just tended. When the necessary work overwhelms the earned enjoyment, a garden that began with high hopes in May produces deep dismay by July.

Between fussy plants, voracious insects, pesky diseases and hysterical weeds, it's easy for a gardener to become overwhelmed with work. So let's underwhelm you. Let's look at all the things you can do to simplify your gardening and minimize your workload, right from the beginning. It's easier than you think. And let's examine ways to make your garden more interesting—and less work—without involving plants at all. Clever use of bricks, gravel, stones and wood can transform a labour-intensive garden into a relaxing paradise without requiring more than a minimum of attention and maintenance.

Somewhere in this world, perhaps, is a gardener who enjoys raking leaves and hoeing weeds, trimming hedges and pruning shrubs, mowing grass and spreading fertilizer, and repeating it day after day during the entire growing season. If you find this person, stay well away—you don't want to catch that sickness!

We say, "Show us a well-used rake and we'll show you an exhausted gardener." When you reach the point when your rake grows rusty while your garden thrives, you discover an entirely new level of joy from gardening.

You're probably making the same mistakes we made.

Some visitors to our garden, including magazine writers and television crews, assume that we're either natural-born gardeners or we were trained in horticulture at an early age. Neither is true. We have completed formal studies in some areas of gardening, but only after we became passionate about it.

We've made as many gardening mistakes as anyone can over thirty years of planting, feeding, watering, and so on. Our thumbs aren't any greener, we suspect, than anyone else's. If they were, we wouldn't have made so many errors over the years.

Our home is not large, but it's located on a substantial lot—about one third of an acre. When we purchased it more than thirty years ago, the rear yard was dotted with fruit trees, remnants of the previous owner's mini-orchard. Aside from the trees, the rest of the yard resembled various foreign lands—a South American jungle in spring, the Gobi Desert in summer, and Baffin Island in winter.

This obviously would not do, so we spent our first ten years and a few thousand dollars attempting to transform the yard into the garden of our dreams. That's when we made most of our mistakes, and they were sometimes embarrassing. So take some satisfaction in learning that most novice gardeners make the same kinds of errors. As long as you learn from your mistakes, it's fine. It can be very reassuring to know, as you survey a clump of withered plants, that others have participated in similar unintentional massacres. Don't give up and don't feel guilty. Look at it this way: If plants could talk, they would let you know the problem. Since they lack vocal chords, the only way they can communicate is either by thriving or by wilting. Hey, is it your fault that a delphinium hasn't evolved as far as your cat has?

The best way to avoid future horticultural massacres is to learn from the mistakes of others before you make them yourselves. That's what much of this book is about.

Let's begin with a combination of True Confessions and Show and Tell. Here are the Ten Biggest Mistakes we made in gardening, along with practical solutions for each. If you've been gardening for a while and have never encountered any of these errors, check the colour of your thumbs. Maybe they're green after all.

MISTAKE #1: LACKING A PLAN

Don't panic. Planning a garden is not like designing a house. It's much easier, more fun and (we hope) substantially less expensive.

You don't need any artistic or architectural talent to create a garden plan. At its most basic, you don't even require a knowledge of plants. Some problems solve themselves just by putting pencil to paper.

When we first grew serious about creating a garden environment, we began with a rough sketch of our house and the location of the flower beds. It looked like this (see "Rough sketch" on page 4).

Making this rough sketch suggested an idea we hadn't thought about before. Why maintain separate flower beds, like islands in a sea of grass? Why not connect them in continuous beds, since the space between them was wasted anyway? The result was our "Modified sketch."

This was a good start and led to other decisions. For example, our garden has a southern exposure, generally a good idea. Besides providing sun for most of the day, it defined the shady areas we would be dealing with. Some plants love the morning sun and fade after lunch; others do well in the heat of the day if other conditions are met (we didn't know this at the time, of course, and you don't have to worry

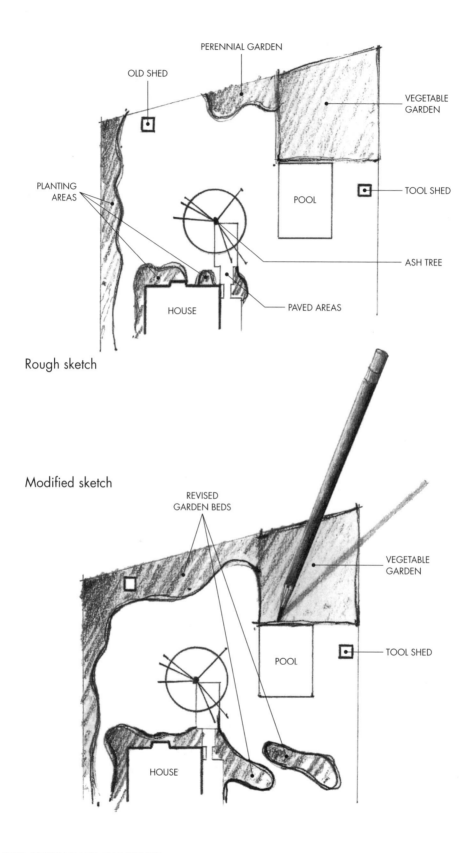

PERENNIAL GARDEN

OLD SHED

VEGETABLE GARDEN

PLANTING AREAS

TOOL SHED

POOL

ASH TREE

HOUSE

PAVED AREAS

Rough sketch

Modified sketch

REVISED GARDEN BEDS

VEGETABLE GARDEN

POOL

TOOL SHED

HOUSE

about it right now). By sketching the shady areas around the house, we helped ourselves decide the location of certain types of plants.

We also saw that it wasn't necessary to fill each and every square foot of space with flowers either, so we identified the best places for flowering shrubs, and filled other spaces with ground-cover plants.

Our home is protected from winds by a nearby escarpment, an advantage many gardens lack. If your garden is subject to strong winds, mark their direction and keep it in mind—some plants, especially ornamental shrubs and specimen trees, don't tolerate wind as well as others.

Next, we took another look at our extended flower beds. This was an improvement, but if our garden were an outdoor living room, it looked as though we were stacking the furniture against all four walls. The most interesting rooms we ever visited contain quiet corners and nooks. Try planning your garden the same way you arrange furniture in your living room. You can even move some plants as often and as frequently as you move your coffee table or easy chairs, if necessary, until you find the perfect location for each.

Assuming we were planning the garden layout we enjoy today, we would have sketched the plan to look something like this:

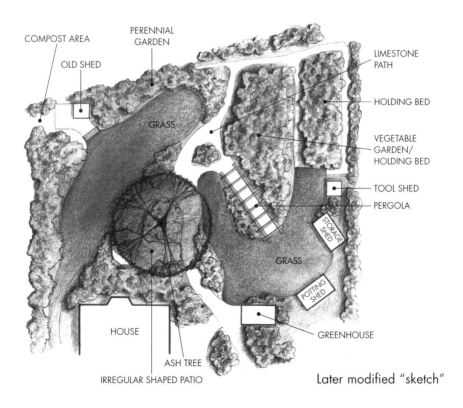

Later modified "sketch"

It would have been impossible to draw a plan such as this when we began, because it took time for our garden to evolve. Over the years a swimming pool, ornamental trees and planting beds have come and gone, and we're always planning new additions or modifications. The road to a perfect garden is endless, and that's part of its appeal to us.

The important step is putting pencil to paper and sketching locations. We suggest you also visit other gardens to see what appeals to you most. We love our pergola and have avoided elevated rock gardens; you may be enraptured by rock gardens and think a pergola is just an overgrown arbour. That's fine with us; the more personal and expressive your garden is, the more enjoyment you'll receive from it. But take a few hours to plan things out, even in the roughest, most basic way. It will save time, money and effort over the years.

One more thing: Before you start any serious planning, read Chapter Two, where we cover garden styles and site assessments.

MISTAKE #2: EXPECTING INSTANT GRATIFICATION

Microwave ovens, air travel and frozen foods have changed the pace of human life, but plants couldn't care less. Rhododendrons still bloom the same two weeks of the year, no one can grow respectable ripe tomatoes in less than eight weeks, and it takes years to establish a garden of perennial flowers.

This is not necessarily A Bad Thing. A garden is an organic creature, and the more time it takes to mature, the longer it can be expected to endure. This doesn't mean you should run your garden according to the same schedule as your retirement plan. But if you are setting out to begin your dream garden environment this spring, don't expect your work of art to peak this year, or even next; look three years ahead, changing course as you go. In other words, try to be patient. As much enjoyment can be gained from the process of creating a garden as from relaxing in it. Best of all, if you plan correctly, you can lessen the effort needed to start your garden, and the work needed to tend it in the future.

A note to parents of grown children: If you're still impatient about enjoying the rewards of your garden sooner rather than later, reflect on how much time you spent on toilet training your youngsters. Creating a garden environment takes about as long . . . but it's more fun for everyone concerned.

MISTAKE #3: BUYING ON IMPULSE

We've all heard stories of people becoming so entranced by a cute puppy in a pet shop window that they take it home only to discover, perhaps a year later, that they are sharing their home with an animal that's a cross between a Great Dane and Godzilla.

Buying a plant or shrub on impulse doesn't produce similar damage, but it's still not such a good idea.

Impulse buying of plants usually begins with: "What beautiful flowers! What interesting foliage! Let's buy one!" Somewhere in your garden, you assure yourself, is the perfect home for this little beauty. But too many things are involved in locating the ideal site for new, unfamiliar plants. Soil quality, moisture and hours of sunlight are some obvious concerns. And what of neighbouring plants? Azaleas and carnations, for example, tolerate each other side by side about as well as two strange tomcats (not to mention that they can look very silly together).

So before visiting a plant nursery, choose a site or two for any new plants you may acquire. Know whether the location is always moist, or subject to dryness; whether it's well shaded, in open shade, partially shaded or in full sun all day long; and which plants already border the site—their height, colour, blooming time and personalities.

The problems of impulse shopping can be even worse when it comes to flowering shrubs. A bridalwreath spirea (*Spirea prunifolia*) can be an eye-catcher when it's in full, delicious bloom during early summer. The rest of the year, the plant is about as interesting as cold mashed potatoes. We're not suggesting you avoid a bridalwreath spirea or any other plant that catches your fancy. But remember that most flowering shrubs have a limited blooming season. When choosing one, think of its effect over fifty weeks of the year, not just two.

MISTAKE #4: NOT PREPARING BEDS BEFORE PLANTING

Another thing about our garden that surprises visitors is the fact that the soil on our property is less than ideal. Much of it is heavy clay and well peppered with rocks. While we eventually learned that most plants can grow in most kinds of soil, we suggest you ward off problems by giving your plants a head start with some soil preparation.

What's with all these Latin names?

Throughout this book, we'll use both the common name (black-eyed Susan) and Latin name (Rudbeckia fulgida) when refer-ring to a specific plant. The Latin names may be unfamiliar and difficult to remember, but they're important to know when you're selecting plants for a specific location. Without referring to the Latin designation, you could be dooming yourself to extra maintenance, and the plant to an early death.

For instance, most people love Clematis, and you may be inspired enough by this book to purchase one for your own garden. But there are over 200 species, deciduous and evergreen, of Clematis to choose from; some do well almost anywhere in Canada, and some cannot tolerate harsh winters east of British Columbia. Some should be pruned severely, some lightly.

Here are a few examples:

Clematis integrifolia is an interesting plant but it's not a climber, blooms in summer and likes its roots moist but in well-drained soil. Clematis lanuginosa "Henryi" will climb ten feet or higher, blooms twice yearly in spring and autumn, requires moist soil conditions and should be pruned back severely in spring. Clematis vitalba blooms in summer only, can become very invasive and prefers dry soil conditions. So if you ask us, "Where should I plant my clematis?" or "When should I prune my clematis?" our reaction is, "Which one?" Each demands different conditions, and it's always necessary to be specific.

Fortunately, you don't have to remember the Latin names for every plant we'll refer to in this book. But we'll include them whenever we speak of a plant's specific characteristics. We have also included space for your List of Favourites on page 174, so you can write the names of plants that appeal to you most, and take this book with you to your garden nursery.

—Dave & Cathy

This is one place where elbow grease cannot be avoided, at least at the outset. But it's a wise investment; a little time spent preparing the soil in your garden beds will save hours of work and buckets of frustration in the future.

MISTAKE #5: LEAVING TOO LITTLE ROOM FOR GROWTH

Remember the old fable about the camel that began by poking its nose in the Bedouin's tent . . . and then its head . . . and then its neck . . . until the camel was entirely in the tent and the Bedouin was out in the cold?

Some trees and shrubs can be like that. The first year, they look cute against the wall of your house. A few years later, your house looks cute sitting in their shadows. Some evergreen trees can be especially a problem. When choosing and planting a tree or shrub, determine how tall it will become at maturity and picture it at full growth in the location you've chosen.

MISTAKE #6: MAKING HIGH-MAINTENANCE CHOICES

Everything in gardening is a trade-off. Some people grow exotic orchids, convinced that the time, effort and investment are worth their extraordinary beauty. Caught up in its splendour, you might choose a plant for its visual appeal first, not caring how much attention it may demand from you.

We think the enjoyment you receive from the plant should match all the effort you invested in growing it. Many species of roses are admittedly beautiful, but are subject to attacks from aphids, mildew and black spot, and all require pruning, deadheading and preparation for winter. Plants such as coral bells (*Heuchera sanguinea*) and purple coneflower (*Echinacea purpurea*) may not have the snooty sophistication of a spectacular hybrid rose, but they're not as prone to tantrums either.

By the way, do you know which plants demand the highest maintenance of all? The answer may come as a shock—they are the grasses that make up your lawn. Nothing else you grow demands more of your time, money, energy and effort—not to mention drinking precious purified water and leaking destructive chemical fertilizers into the environment—than your acreage of grass. (Stay calm; we have some solid suggestions in Chapter Six.)

MISTAKE #7: PUTTING YOUR PLANTS IN PLATOONS

Plants make lousy soldiers. Most can't stand perfectly straight, they grow in varying heights, and they don't take orders very well. Yet many beginning gardeners, including us a decade or two ago, insist on arranging plants like soldiers on parade with little foot soldiers in the front, normal-sized in the middle, and giant generals at the rear.

Remember that gardens are organic, and organic life tends to be messy, confused and bordering on chaotic; in fact, these qualities are part of its charm. So avoid thinking like a drill sergeant when setting out plants. Don't base their position strictly according to height. There are too many other qualities to consider, including bloom colour, soil conditions, watering needs, sun and shade.

MISTAKE #8: THINKING TOO SMALL

When we began to garden, but before we learned the Rusty Rake secrets, we kept our flower beds small, assuming they would require less maintenance, and filled them with familiar annuals such as marigolds and petunias.

Unfortunately, there's nothing very attractive about several postage-stamp flower beds scattered among the grass, no matter how healthy the plants may be. By concentrating our selection on flowering annuals, plus nurturing all that expanse of lawn around them, we were expending more energy than it was worth.

Only when we enlarged our flower beds, established our perennials, focused on low-maintenance plants, made use of ground covers and shrubs, discovered the value of mulches, and added nooks and corners did our garden become truly satisfying and worth the effort.

Try for a balance between the area available in your garden, the size of your plantings and beds, and your ability to care for your plants using Rusty Rake ideas. Once again, think of your garden as a room, with a balance between open "floor" (your lawn and other ground cover), "furniture" (the flower beds and shrub plantings) and "walls" (trees and tall grasses).

MISTAKE #9: HAVING A "FAST FOOD" APPETITE

Maybe this individual sounds familiar to you:

Each May 24th weekend, this person drives to the local garden nursery, pays top dollar for flats of pansies, petunias and impatiens, tosses them in the car, drives home, spends the weekend sticking them in the soil, spends every weekend until Thanksgiving watering the little devils, and after the first frost yanks them out of the ground and tosses them onto the compost heap. This is not a Rusty Rake gardener.

We have nothing against annuals; we love growing them as container plants to add colour to a patio or porch. We also like cheeseburgers and French fries, but we haven't made a steady diet of them since we left our teenage years behind.

Most bedding annuals are the horticultural equivalent of fast food: you drive up, gulp it down and feel satisfied. Then you do it all over again the next time. It's a form of instant gratification.

But annuals tend to be high-maintenance plants. Petunias and marigolds require frequent deadheading to promote new blooms, and their shallow roots demand water and food all through the summer growing season.

We think a more satisfying approach is to take a long-term view by maximizing the number of perennials in your garden. They may not be in bloom when you purchase them; they may not even bloom the first season at all. But they return your investment year after year with little care, and they tend to be more interesting and pleasurable than everyday annuals.

Instead of filling a shady area exclusively with impatiens (which you have to replace every spring), break up the monotony with shade-tolerant perennials such as bleeding heart (*Dicentra spectabilis*), hosta, astilbe or ferns. In hot sunny areas, consider black-eyed Susans (*Rudbeckia fulgida*), blanket flower (*Gaillardia*), stonecrop (*Sedum*) or silver sage (*Artemesia ludoviciana*). All are low-maintenance choices with interesting shapes and habits, and all will return faithfully year after year instead of hightailing it to the compost heap with the first frost of autumn.

MISTAKE #10: EXPECTING PERFECTION

Here's a test:

Try to recall the most comfortable room you have ever entered—one that invited you to sit, relax and spend as much time in it as you wanted. It may have been in a country bed-and-breakfast, or at a friend's apartment. Wherever it was, we'll bet it was not furnished like a display window in an upscale home-decorating store, where everything is coordinated and the sofa cushions look as though they have never been sat upon. We also expect that the carpet might have been frayed a little, the furniture wasn't all from the same manufacturer or even the same period, and the walls were decorated with quirky pictures and accessories. Most of all, it was probably an informal room, not a parlour at Versailles.

If you think of your garden as a comfortable and inviting room in your house, you shouldn't expect it to have a pristine appearance either. Not all your plants will be in bloom at the same time, the lilies won't be quite where you'd prefer them, and your Japanese maple may be overdue for a haircut.

So what? Are you comfortable? Are your guests comfortable? Does the beauty of your flower beds dominate your urge to rise from your chair and tidy up the border plants? Is your garden more suitable for wearing shorts and a T-shirt than a slinky black dress or an ascot?

When you can answer "Yes!" to all of these questions, you're enjoying your garden the way it was meant to be enjoyed, and it starts by rejecting the whole concept of perfectionism.

If you can't shake this idea of a perfect garden setting, with flowers at the peak of their blooming cycle all season long, then we have the same word for you that the man gave Dustin Hoffman in *The Graduate*:

Plastic.

Running your garden instead of it running you

Now that we've shared our mistakes, it's time to offer some actions you can take to establish who's the boss in your garden, no matter what its stage of development may be. These are broad suggestions only; complete details are coming up in later chapters.

ACTION #1: START VISITING OTHER GARDENS

Most of the ideas you'll ever need to truly enjoy your garden already exist—somewhere else.

Books and magazines are a great resource, of course. But for scale, layout, arrangement and overall environment, nothing beats visits to local gardens to absorb new ideas. Many private gardens are included in garden tours for charitable causes or social functions. Seek them out, absorb what the gardeners and landscape designers have done, and apply your imagination.

Notice that we said "visits." When you discover a garden that seems to capture the mood you would like to create around your own home, plan to return as frequently as possible during the growing season. This is not practical for private gardens, of course. Even the friendliest gardener is likely to grow a little annoyed by your fourth or fifth visit.

Most communities in Canada have public gardens, and they'll teach you a good deal about planning and plant selection. If the public gardens in your area are uninspiring, or if you have borrowed every appealing and practical idea from them you can use, try looking further afield. We're fortunate that one of the finest gardens in the world, the Royal Botanical Gardens near Hamilton, is practically a neighbour of ours. But we also seek out other spectacular gardens, setting them as destinations for summer vacation trips.

Books such as this one and magazine articles are helpful, but they can't totally replace tours of actual gardens. Try to locate a few in your area. Be sure to visit them, if possible, in fall and winter as well. Your garden is a year-round presence, and it's possible to improve its February appearance with a little planning in April.

ACTION #2: DON'T MESS WITH MOTHER NATURE TOO MUCH

Gardeners have been finding ways to adapt plants for different climates over the past thousand years or more. Many of our favourite plants originated far beyond North American shores, in places such as the Mediterranean and Asia, and their cultivar offspring are now as contented here as many native plants.

But Mother Nature can be pushed only so far. When some plants are forced to survive in alien conditions, they begin demanding extra attention from you—attention you should try to avoid.

This doesn't always concern species from foreign lands, by the way. It can happen with any plant unable to adapt to a climate radically different from the one in which it evolved.

Consider the birch tree (*Betula papyrifera*), that favourite of suburban southern Ontario. All self-respecting suburban developers in southern Ontario include a clump of birches in every illustration of their split-level paradise. Everyone loves the idea of birches in their yard, where the tree's white trunks and graceful branches are a pleasant sight all year round. Everyone, that is, except the birches.

Birch trees evolved in much colder, drier weather than they encounter in most Canadian suburbs. It's too much to expect a birch to thrive in suburban soil through a long, hot southern Canadian summer. Nothing in its genetics prepares it for the climate. What's more, pests such as the birch leaf miner, which the tree can shrug off in colder climates, run rampant in hot weather, turning the leaves brown and encouraging people to treat the tree with a potent foul-smelling pesticide, which damages the environment and launches its own chain of problems.

The more plants you choose that are native to, or have adapted to, conditions in your garden, the less you'll have to worry about their well-being. We suggest you focus on them (there's a whole list coming), and use more exotic species like condiments to add a little spice and mystery.

ACTION #3: CORRAL RAMBUNCTIOUS MEMBERS

One of the terms you'll hear frequently on these pages is "invasive." We tend to associate this term with weeds, but popular plants can become aggressive as well. Some ornamental grasses, for example, look great as a single clump but resemble a miniature jungle when allowed to spread unchecked. Spectacular flowers, such as black-eyed Susan, are welcomed in almost any garden, but not in every location where they find fertile soil.

Keeping invasive plants at bay is relatively easy with a little prevention. Plants that spread via underground rhizomes, such as many grasses, should be kept inside plastic pots with the bottoms removed. They'll get all the nourishment they need and their wandering habits will be controlled.

Tricks like these keep plants from running amok with just a little preparation.

ACTION #4: STOP DOING WHAT YOU HATE DOING!

Here's our totally unscientific list of the things that most gardeners enjoy the least:

1. Pruning—trees, shrubs, hedges.
2. Fertilizing the lawn.
3. Mowing the lawn.

How do you cut down the amount of time needed to perform these chores? We suggest you stop treating the effect and start treating the cause.

Deadheading: A quick definition

Removing spent blossoms from plants—both annuals and perennials—prevents them from going to seed and encourages new flowers. This is "deadheading," and it improves the overall appearance of your garden.

There's no special trick to the process (but with geraniums and similar plants with long-stemmed flowers, remember to pinch off both stem and flower), and as long as there isn't an over-whelming amount to do, deadheading can be a pleasant task on a sunny day. Use either scissors or thumb and forefinger. Generally, the less deadheading your flowers need, the more you'll enjoy your garden.

—Cathy & Dave

You perform these chores because you have plants that demand them—especially fruit trees and privet hedges. Forsythia looks terrific for two weeks in April, then it spends the rest of the summer reaching for the sky, or at least beyond the reach of your pruners.

Do you honestly need a shrub that demands you stand on a ladder in order to lop off its head every few weeks? Is a privet hedge the only way to mark the boundary of your driveway or yard? Can you do without an expanse of lawn large enough to cover Flin Flon? We're not proposing you convert your lawn to a mini-desert, or even to eliminate grass completely. But try to imagine areas of your garden where attractive ground-cover plants such as Japanese spurge (*Pachysandra terminalis*) would look just as attractive and rarely need cutting, feeding, weeding or (except in unusual circumstances) watering. Combine some good ground cover with a few attractive shrubs and you could quickly elim-inate a hundred square feet or more of grass—and never miss it.

Start thinking about banishing some of that high-maintenance lawn now, and we'll provide some other attractive alternatives later.

ACTION #5: PAY ATTENTION TO DARWIN

Charles D. got it right 150 years ago when he discovered the concept of survival of the fittest. Why not apply his theory to your perennial garden? After preparing the soil and choosing the location of your plants, let them determine their future to some extent. They require some attention until they're established, but don't overdo it. Excessive feeding, fussing and attention produces dependency in plants every bit as much as it does in children.

This is another good reason to focus your attention on perennials. Unlike annuals, perennials plan on hanging around for a few years, so they set their roots deeply in the ground. When drought season arrives and annuals are gasping to be watered daily by you—who else?—perennials are contentedly drinking from moisture deep within the soil.

There's more: The deeper roots of perennials mean they can draw nourishment from wider sources than wimpy annuals. Most annuals demand a liquid feeding every week or two all during the summer. But a dressing of compost each spring is usually enough to see most perennials through the year, leaving you time for other things. Like playing tennis. Or singing. Or reading gardening books . . .

Puttering is fun.
Work is...work.

We're not suggesting a totally passive approach to gardening, by any means. While some folks may be sufficiently lazy or wealthy to hire professionals who create and tend their gardens, that's not our goal. We enjoy puttering in the garden, experimenting with new plants, encouraging reluctant members, and watching the garden evolve season by season, year by year.

The difference between puttering at things you enjoy in the garden and performing high-maintenance chores is similar to the difference between painting your house and painting a landscape or portrait. Both involve a brush and paint, but one is a burden and the other is creative fun.

We admit it—we'll choose creativity and fun over chores any day!

This book helps you do the same, by minimizing the work you need to enjoy plants and other elements in your garden. Frequent short puttering sessions are more fun, and usually more effective, than a weekend-long marathon spent trying to harness your garden's descent into chaos and madness.

Finally: Everyone thinks of gardening in the spring. It's only natural. But many of the ideas we've gathered for this book can be performed during other seasons. Preparing soil, moving perennials (but do it early!) and adding permanent materials such as stones or bricks can all be performed in fall. The idea is to spread your gardening activity across as many months as possible.

If you have felt dominated by your garden in the past, or if an empty expanse of lawn has defied you to create the kind of garden area you desire, open the window, stick your head out and yell at your plants, "I'm going to create the garden of my dreams and none of you is going to stop me!"

Or just pour yourself a cup of tea and go on to the next chapter...

Words of wisdom from a practical man

We made many mistakes when we began—including the mistake of believing plants were more important than they should be.

The previous owner of our home had nurtured some fruit trees, probably remnants of a working orchard. We had few other plants in our yard, so we assumed something of a foster-parent attitude to the trees. Since we had inherited them, we felt responsible for their well-being. After all, the trees had stood for at least ten years under the care of the previous owner. Didn't they deserve the same attention from us?

But here's what we didn't know about fruit trees:
1. They live fast and die young. Fruit trees have a productive life of between 15 and 20 years. Once they're past that age they just stand around getting grey-haired and wrinkled, complaining about the younger generation and longing for The Good Old Days.
2. Fruit trees are about as high maintenance as you can tackle. They demand feeding, pruning, spraying and other time-consuming and expensive pampering.
3. Cherry trees are especially prone to black-knot problems as they grow old (black-knot attacks are like a severe case of bark-acne to a tree). Peach trees become infested with peach borers who gnaw away at various living parts of the plant.

For years, we coddled those ungrateful devils, removing their black knots, pruning their limbs, spraying for borers and generally trying to extend their miserable lives. We managed to harvest just enough cherries and peaches each year for Cathy to bake a few pies, and practically begged the trees to look nice when guests arrived. None of it worked. They kept drooping, declining and decaying.

Convinced we were doing something wrong, we described our problem to a farmer friend who dropped in for a visit one day. "What should we do?" we asked.

He scowled at the trees, then looked back at us as though we had asked if it's a good idea to come in out of the rain. "Cut 'em down!" he said without hesitation. "Take 'em out and plant something new, something that won't give you so much trouble!"

We took his advice. Now we buy the cherries and peaches for Cathy's pies at the market, and Dave has a supply of well-aged cherry wood in the basement for some future woodworking projects.

No, we don't feel guilty. And we don't miss them a bit.

—Dave & Cathy

CHAPTER 2

WHEN DO WE START HAVING FUN?

Of all the things in and around your home, a garden seems like the least essential component. Every Canadian home needs protection from the weather, sources of light and heat, running water, places to eat and sleep, bathroom facilities, and so on. Nothing says it needs a garden filled with shrubs and blooming plants.

But all these practical items in a home exist to meet the body's needs. A garden—whether it's a rambling expanse, a suburban plot or an inner-city courtyard—exists to meet the needs of the soul. Its purpose is to provide comfort, beauty and joy.

Some people lose sight of this idea. They seem to tend their garden for the same reasons their grandparents chopped firewood—because it is an essential chore, performed with a sense of stern duty and avoided at one's peril.

We won't pretend that a successful garden doesn't make demands on its owners. Of course it does. The real secret to enjoying a garden is to harvest enough satisfaction from your garden that you forget all the effort put into it. When your reward, measured in beauty and satisfaction, no longer matches your effort, something is wrong. Puttering becomes replaced with drudgery, and a stroll in the garden becomes an immersion in guilt.

You may not have reached this point yet. You may be simply planning to establish a new garden or overhaul an existing one. Or you may be discovering that the roles are becoming reversed with time, and your garden is beginning to run your life instead of the other way around.

So let's take a methodical approach to your garden, by defining a) what you have; b) what you want; and c) how to achieve it with maximum fun and minimum toil.

Are you in the country, in the city or somewhere in between?

Rural gardens and city gardens have different roles to play, and it's not simply a matter of relative size.

A successful country garden usually becomes more integrated with its surroundings than a small city garden. A country-dweller's garden is often defined by natural or almost-natural boundaries such as streams, ditches, rambling fences, woodlots and mature trees. The shape, as a result, can be almost whatever the gardener determines, and its role includes meeting the needs not only of the gardener but also of surrounding plants and wildlife.

Urban gardens, often courtyard areas, are defined by exterior walls and inflexible fences, making them fixed and rectangular in shape. As a result, urban gardens tend to be very specific extensions of the home, like open-air parlours.

Suburban gardens, such as our own, are naturally somewhere in the middle. They offer the gardener a little of both worlds, which can often be their downfall because they ask for a decision to be made. Will your garden extend the country to your back door or be an annex to your house?

These are not inflexible decisions, but they provide a benchmark when planning your garden. It also helps to remember this concept when you can't determine just what it is about your garden that troubles you. People will often succeed in establishing and raising plants in their garden, but feel that somehow "it just doesn't work." It may not work because you may be expecting a different function for your garden area. Which leads to:

Do you prefer formality or informality?

Formal gardens evolved in Europe during the sixteenth and seventeenth centuries when wealthy rural landowners set out to impose civilized behaviour on the wilderness around them. The wildness of nature was banished behind high stone walls and thick hedges, and the lines of the gardens within them were either precisely straight or set in complex geometric patterns. It was a form of horticultural architecture, with more emphasis on the fixed designs than on the plants themselves.

Middle-class Europeans (especially the British), a class that emerged in the mid-nineteenth century, began to copy many lifestyles of the upper classes, including their preference for formal garden layouts, and we have been dealing with their influence ever since. This is how we ended up with clipped hedges, expansive lawns and straight-line flower beds.

Formal gardens can be pleasant places, as anyone who has visited some of England's most famous gardens will agree. But the greater the formality, the more work is needed to keep things that way. Some suburban gardeners still seem to feel that at least one function of a garden is to demonstrate that the owner has conquered the surrounding "wilderness"—thus manicured hedges, rigid boundaries and sharply defined flower beds.

Fortunately, there has been a move toward informality for many years, and it has gained real momentum in urban and suburban areas of North America. Informal gardens are, in our opinion, more relaxing to the eye and more expressive of the owner than any formal layout.

The more informal your garden is, the fewer demands it is likely to place on you for chores. So wherever possible, if you strive for a natural, less formal mood in your garden you'll discover much more time to enjoy it.

Do you want a shady, peaceful retreat or colour throughout the growing season?

This decision makes a major impact on the kinds of plants you choose and where you place them.

We prefer colour, so we arranged our beds to show off blooms as much as possible, and maintained large open spaces for the sun to reach them. But we have also visited gardens that are intentionally shaded and cool, with the emphasis on lush green vegetation instead of riotous colour. Shady gardens can be delightful, a little mysterious and naturally "air-conditioned" during summer heat.

Each is not exclusive of the other. We maintain a couple of shady nooks in our garden, and a shady garden can grow blooms here and there to break up the greenery. But it's worth asking yourself which type of garden appeals to you most when you're still at the planning stage.

Are you making a new garden or changing an existing one?

The rules don't differ very much between these two choices, except when it comes to the plants you may wish to keep from an existing garden. Base your decisions on these three guidelines (and we're talking perennials here, of course):

> • Do you have any favourite plants that are doing well and you wish to keep them in your new garden layout? If you do choose a new location for them, make sure it is suitable for their needs (shade or sun, damp or dry soil, etc.). With care, some small perennials can be moved successfully during the growing season if the roots are undisturbed, but it's best to tackle this in the early spring or in the autumn, when active growth has ceased. We prefer spring, because it gives the plants the entire growing season to re-establish a good root system.
> • Are some plants you value languishing because they're in the wrong location? Again, it's a matter of more or less sun, shade and moisture. Interestingly enough, the happier a plant is in its location, the less maintenance it often requires. So you can reduce your workload with current plants in your garden simply by finding a better spot for them.
> • Are older plants in the wrong place, or don't suit your new garden layout? Shrubs and small trees that have resided in the same location for five years or more will have a large, well-developed root system that defies moving the plant without expert professional help. We suggest you attempt to move them only as a last resort. Try building them into your new garden plan, if at all possible.

Walk before you dig

All gardens, even small inner-city sites, are subject to varying levels of sun, shade and moisture as well as different soil types. A little time spent walking slowly around your garden plot with pencil, paper and trowel will help you in your planning and avoid potential disaster later on.

For example, a shady corner of your garden where the soil is loamy and always damp will be perfect for ferns, but forget about growing poppies there. Similarly, well-drained sandy soil in a place that receives a full day of sun may suit carnations fine, but will be fatal to rhododendrons.

How low can you go? Apparently not low enough.

Before you decide to move any well-established plants around, here's a cautionary tale:

With great confidence in our skills—and Dave's strength—we decided one year to move two attractive yew shrubs. They had been growing in the same location, we estimated, for about twenty years. They were barely two feet tall, and would look much more attractive in a special corner of the garden. So one morning, Dave went to work with the garden spade, digging beneath their roots.

By lunch he was still digging. And almost disappearing in the massive hole. These yews had a root system that would have done justice to a sequoia!

Finally Dave managed to clear all the earth away from the root ball, carefully transported them to their new, specially prepared location, set them in place and pampered them with water, special fertilizers and a prayer or two.

They died anyway.

—Cathy & Dave

Whenever you encounter different levels of moisture in your garden, mark the location on your sketch. Estimate how much sun each receives during the growing season, and which locations are either sheltered from, or susceptible to, strong winds. Now you have two choices: Select plants to match the characteristics of the various locations, or change the characteristics to match the plants you want to grow there.

You can change many aspects of a location, but they all involve time-consuming and expensive effort. Sandy soil can be removed and replaced with loam or clay, damp areas can be drained and sunny corners can be shaded with fencing or shrubs. It's not so difficult to modify the soil a little as well, by adding loam to sandy soil for nutrients, sand to heavy clay soils to break them up, and good old peat moss to any kind of soil as a conditioner. But unless your garden site is impossible—and very few are—make an attempt to match the plants to the soil and light conditions, not vice versa.

Moving techniques for established plants

You can improve your chances of success when moving a well-established plant by following these steps:

1. Choose a cool, damp day to move plants. They have a better chance of surviving the shock under these conditions than on excessively hot days.
2. Heavily soak the soil all around the plant (in its current location). In most cases, wet an area about the same diameter as the lower branches of the plant. Don't be afraid to overdo it.
3. Prepare the new site for the plant by digging a hole that is several inches wider and deeper than the size of the plant's root ball.

Dig a hole twice as wide and at least half again as deep as the plant's root ball. Mix peat moss, compost and excavated soil, and place beneath the plant to elevate it.

4. It's a good idea to add peat moss and organic matter (preferably compost) to the excavated soil and mix thoroughly. If you are working with heavy soil, chip the sides and bottom of the new hole with your spade, then work in a little peat moss and compost material. This gives the roots a better chance to establish themselves.

5. Dig carefully around and under the root system of the plant, using the lower branches as a guide (usually roots don't extend beyond the perimeter of the widest branches).

6. Lift the plant out on the shovel, transport it to the new location, and measure the depth from the bottom of the root ball to the spot where the plant emerges from the ground. Adjust the depth of the new hole to match this, and set the plant in its new home.

7. Fill the hole with the prepared mixture and tamp the soil firmly around the plant. Adding a transplant-type fertilizer is optional, but we think it's a good idea. We prefer water-soluble types, such as 10-52-10; mix as directed by the manufacturer, and water the plant thoroughly with the mixture. If you prefer to use a granular type of fertilizer, be sure it has a high phosphate content (the second number) such as Superphosphate. Work this into the surface of the soil around the plant and water thoroughly.

Do you know your hardiness zone?

Hardiness zones were created to guide plant growers on the types of plants best suited for local climates. It's not strictly necessary to know the precise zone limits in your area, because a quick glance at your neighbour's gardens or a visit to a local nursery will indicate the types of plants suited to your local climate. What's more, zones are merely a guide to growers; many areas have microclimates, which are pockets that are warmer or colder than other areas. A microclimate may be as large as a township or as small as your own yard. For example, a garden at the bottom of a valley or atop a high escarpment is likely to receive frost later in the spring and earlier in the fall than nearby gardens at different elevations. And gardens on a slope facing south may enjoy a substantially longer growing season than others. Gardens in the centre of towns and cities also tend to be slightly warmer than those in the adjacent countryside. Canadian zones range from 1 to 9; the higher the number, the milder the climate. U.S. zones range from 1 to 10.

The most important point to remember is that Canadian hardiness zones, which were established by Agriculture Canada in 1967, are different from those used in the United States. The difference is an entire zone; under the U.S. system, the western end of Lake Ontario (where we reside) is in Zone 5, but Agricultural Canada defines it as Zone 6. Canadian zone limits are more detailed as well. U.S. zone maps identify almost all of Vancouver Island as Zone 8, but it actually ranges from

Zones 2 to 9. Keep this in mind if you refer to American gardening books, or if you purchase plants imported from the United States that come with a hardiness zone guide. Make sure the guide number refers to Canadian zones, not American ones.

Hardier plant types are being developed year by year, and some species once considered impossible to grow successfully in harsh areas are now commonplace in those regions.

What do you want to see in your garden?
What do you want to hide?

Rural and suburban gardens often look out upon various neighbouring structures or features, and good planning can either include them in your garden environment or exclude them from your sight. In many cases, their presence can suggest locations for large shade trees or shrubs.

For example, if your neighbours have an especially attractive and highly visible tree in their yard—perhaps a weeping willow, or a red maple that explodes with colour each fall—you may want to keep it in sight for your enjoyment as well. We call this a "borrowed view," and it can add to the beauty of your garden without requiring any effort from you, such as dealing with those pesky willow roots, or gathering the maple's leaves when they drop. Similarly, the sight of a picturesque distant hill, or a lake or river on the horizon can be borrowed views. If they appeal to you, try not to hide them with trees or shrubs when making your plan.

The opposite of a borrowed view is a banished one—a sight you prefer not to include in your garden's vista, such as an ugly fence, a tall building or your neighbour's drab garden shed. When you can see these intrusions from a centralized part of your garden, conceal them behind well-placed shrubs such as lilacs, or place ivy-covered trellises and lattice fences on the perimeter of your property.

Here's another hint about borrowed and banished views:

As Canadians, we spend at least a third of the year looking at our garden from inside the house. From November to March, not much happens above ground, but the view remains nevertheless. Birds and animals visit, and under a blanket of fresh snow our yard assumes a new kind of beauty. There's a special quality to garden design that can only be appreciated during late fall and winter, and since this amounts

"Good bones" make your garden interesting even in the dead of winter.

to at least two or three months of the year, it's worth taking into consideration.

Gardens that look good year-round are said to have "good bones." This means they are attractive and interesting even when the annuals have died off, the perennials are dormant, and the deciduous trees have lost all their leaves. What's the secret of good bones? Balance helps; the overall view should be interesting, with no empty spaces here or there. Since there is little or no colour, your eye should be attracted to shapes, textures and lines. Here are a few items that add these qualities to a garden all year round, and really prove their worth during the dormant months:

- Meandering flagstone, brick or pebble-stone pathways;
- Stone or concrete statuary, columns, sundials, etc.;
- Cedar benches that age in the weather;
- Arbours, pergolas and wooden screens;
- Evergreens (but choose and place them carefully; they have a habit of outgrowing their surroundings, and too many can create a sombre, formal mood in your garden);
- Interesting deciduous plants such as corkscrew Hazel (*Corylus avellana* 'Contorta'—sometimes also called Harry Lauder's walking stick) that attract the eye even when their leaves have dropped;

- Ornamental grasses that maintain their foliage through the winter;
- Garden sheds—try to choose well-designed wooden structures, not metal or plastic.

We wish we could tell you where to place each of these elements for the best effect, but we can't. Everyone's garden is, and should be, unique. Your tastes and interests are different from those of anyone else. With variables such as the location, size, shape and setting of your garden, it becomes impossible to establish any kind of fixed formula. Instead, we can offer these suggestions:

- Mix different textures—the grey patina of weathered cedar, the rough surface of granite rocks, the washboard surface of a pebbled walkway.
- Keep the colours as natural as possible. We choose natural wood or wood stains over painted surfaces. White and brilliant red are beautiful and dramatic, but they add a more formal mood to a garden than we prefer. They also require more maintenance.
- Avoid straight lines and small curves in large garden properties. Paths should meander, and flower beds should either follow the natural shape of your property or be shaped in long, graceful bends.
- Wherever possible, reduce the lawn area. Unless you plan to use a section of your garden for croquet, badminton or polo you need no more than one third of your total garden area as a lawn . . . and maybe even less.
- Remember that a garden is a four-season area. Some plants you choose can add interest, no matter what season it may be. Dogwood and other shrubs, for example, display bright red branches to the world all winter after shedding their leaves, so one or two of these plants in appropriate locations of your garden become a source of colour on dull winter days.
- Add an attractive bird feeder or two. Daily visits from jays, chicka-dees, cardinals and other birds that winter in most parts of Canada will literally add life to your garden during the dull winter months. Remember to keep the feeders filled with seed; the birds will come to depend on you. The birds will scatter seeds, which could lead to a crop of unwanted plants come spring. We reduce the problem by planting a ground cover of Lambs' Ears (*Stachys byzantina*) beneath the feeders, reducing the number of seeds that sprout. You could use almost any thick perennial ground cover.
- Experiment. All gardens are a work in progress, including the "bones" you add to yours.

Garbage cans are evergreens,
brooms are trees, hoses are borders

Here's a silly idea that has saved us hours of toil and frustration when planning a garden:

Before you buy and plant shrubs, ornamental trees and other additions to your garden, use some "stand-ins" and your imagination. Picture an overturned (and empty, of course) garbage can as a shrub or large plant, and brooms, rakes and shovels as low trees. Then position each around your garden until their locations please your eye. At our place, this usually consists of one person standing at the window or in the centre of the garden directing the other person with hand gestures and instructions such as "Back about a foot . . . now over to your right . . ." When you've finally located the final location of each, mark it and dig. This is much easier on both you and the plant than constantly moving it around, digging up and burying the roots over and over again until it looks "just right."

Here's another suggestion:

When laying out new flower beds, use a garden hose to mark the boundaries before you dig. A hose is perfect for marking the long, slow curves we like to see in large flower beds, and you won't be digging and backfilling if you make an error.

Apply a little creativity and
save a large shrub

Many suburban homeowners who planted small junipers against their house or in their garden ten or fifteen years ago must now deal with shrubs as big as Buicks. Often the shrub has lost its appeal or its suitability for the site, and it may be far too large to relocate. Instead of removing it entirely, try shaping it bonsai-style. Trim small branches and lower growth, exposing the interesting pattern of main branches and leaving greenery at the top. Set an attractive mulch or ground cover around its base. Most healthy evergreens and other shrubs can be shaped in this manner.

Make your garden an environment,
not an amphitheatre

We're fortunate (or is it cursed?) with a larger-than-average sized property. But no matter what the size of your garden may be, it's a good

Try Bonsai-style pruning to add interest to dull, oversized shrubs. Emphasize or develop an S-curve in the trunk, as shown in the bottom sketch.

idea to try breaking the space into separate nooks or small "rooms." A garden that does not reveal itself to you all at once, but invites you to explore its many different corners, is appealing and enchanting. This matches our preference for meandering pathways, individual groupings, and trees and structures to provide "bones." It also makes tackling a new garden, or a major make-over, a little less daunting, since you can work on one small area at a time.

Instead of surveying the entire garden as one massive space to be developed, see it as a layout for an open-air home. Picture an

entertainment area—large enough to accommodate a table for guests, perhaps shaded from the hot afternoon sun. Connect it to two or three "parlours." One parlour could be a striking specimen tree surrounded by perennials, another could include a bench set in front of a screen supporting ivy or clematis, and a third could be a rock garden or other grouping. These will take time to establish, but they are also compact enough for you to focus upon just one each year, building your

environment bit by bit. They also reduce maintenance, because they tend to be more accessible than oversized mass plantings.

One more time: Be patient and prudent

We have found that brusque and demanding people have little interest in gardening. Good thing too, we say. Executives who thump their desks and bark "I want it done now!" become totally frustrated by plants that operate on their own schedule, thank you very much.

Keep this in mind when planning your garden, and don't try to rush things. If you're a beginning gardener, or if you're out to create a garden environment from an open expanse of lawn, limit your sights a little for the first year or two. Better to have a small area that works, and provides some valuable experience, than trying to transform an expanse of shrubs and flowers that soon gets out of control.

How to simplify by thinking ahead

When we talk about simplifying your garden plans, we don't mean your garden has to be boring and one-dimensional. We mean thinking ahead to avoid complications and extra work. Here are some suggestions:

> • Think ahead when planning the size of flower beds and paths. In smaller gardens, try to keep plant beds wide enough to group the plants but narrow enough for you to work easily among them. We think 5 to 10 feet is fine. Paths shouldn't be less than 2 feet wide for standing. (Remember that you may be carrying tools when you're treading the pathways.) If you'll be kneeling at your plants—we trust for puttering, not praying they'll stay alive—make them about 2-1/2 to 3 feet wide. If you're trundling a cart down a pathway, set it about 4 feet wide. Small planning considerations such as these will cut time, trouble and frustration later when your plants are established.
> • Make it easy to reach your plants. Try to set deep beds against a fence, leaving a pathway between the rear line of plants and the fence structure so you can reach them easily. We use flat stepping stones between the plants, providing dry access to the centre of the beds.
> • You don't really need wall-to-wall (or fence-to-fence) flower beds in your garden. Ground cover and mulch can add attractive maintenance-free areas to set off individual beds or frame dramatic shrubs.

• Eliminate or at least reduce predictable chores. Planting a lone tree in the centre of a grassy area won't do much either for the tree's appearance or the health of the grass. Instead, construct a bed beneath the tree and plant it with low-care ground cover such as periwinkle. Trimming is required less frequently around ground cover. You also reduce the risk of striking the tree with the mower, which can create potential health problems. Best of all, you'll be reducing the total area of grass to be fed, watered and cut—and that's a Rusty Rake Gardener objective.

• Compost is the sacred lifeblood of our garden. It nurtures the perennials, reduces our volume of garbage and probably qualifies everyone who believes in it for sainthood. We generate a good deal of raw material for compost, but instead of maintaining one massive pile, we've separated them into three locations. One is handy to the back door, making it convenient to scurry outside with kitchen scraps in mid-winter. The other two are hidden behind shrubs in the garden itself, so it's a short walk to them during the growing season when we're pruning, removing dead leaves or just puttering. By all means, plan to have at least one compost heap, and think ahead to locate it in the place where it is easy to reach no matter what you are doing.

• We'll deal with this subject in detail later, but never underestimate the value of mulch. It retains moisture in the soil, inhibits weeds, nurtures the plants, looks terrific and, for all we know, it might even prevent tooth decay. It's a very simple idea that can make a very big difference in reducing your gardening chores.

• Schedule daily "walkabouts" in your garden to admire/inspect the plants, snatch away any weeds and deadhead flowers. Some people love doing this early in the morning, with their first cup of coffee in hand. You choose the time; the idea is to perform these little duties for a few minutes each day, when they're fun, instead of once a week, when they can become an overwhelming task.

Some kids have no sense of aesthetics

Early in our gardening career, we got very caught up with the idea of creating special environments, including the construction of raised beds to lift plantings above the flat surface of our lawn.

One spring day, Dave set out with a few wheelbarrows full of topsoil, a spade and a rough idea of what he wanted to do.

He began by creating a low oval-shaped hillock of top soil perhaps 8 feet long and 3 feet wide. It looked so good that he extended two narrow beds from each end to create a wide U-shaped pattern. This worked well, except that a long, open, triangular shape remained at a third corner, set between two walkways, so he piled dirt there as well. Now he had a kind of free-form shape, and he stood leaning on his shovel and considering what to plant in his new elevated-bed creation.

At this point, a young neighbourhood boy happened to pass by. Seeing Dave standing there looking smug in front of the newly piled dirt, the boy stopped and stared. Then he approached for a closer look, studied Dave's handiwork, and finally said in a perfectly honest and somewhat confused voice: "How come you buried a horse in your front lawn, mister?"

Dave looked at him curiously, then back at his new raised-bed design. The kid was right. It looked as though Northern Dancer had been interred near the end of our driveway—body, legs, neck and all.

Dave politely suggested the boy should be in school or at least playing hooky, and quickly redesigned our newest garden plot.

—Cathy

CHAPTER 3

SOME PLANTS HAVE TIME
TO WASTE. YOURS.

No one falls in love with a plant just because it requires little or no maintenance. In our experience, people choose plants for a host of other perfectly acceptable reasons, beginning with their beauty—colour, shape, aroma, etc.—and other motives such as:

- "We've always grown (roses, petunias, delphiniums, etc.)"
- "Look what's on sale!"
- "I saw one of those in a garden down the street yesterday."
- "I've never seen a plant like that before—I've got to have it!"
- "This will look nice in that empty corner of the garden."

We're familiar with these words because we've spoken them ourselves and lived to regret them . . . but not lately.

Unless you have a good deal of time, experience and energy, we suggest you limit yourself at the beginning to plants that are easy-going, independent and reliable. Then, when you're comfortable with your basic garden, you can begin adding plants that require a little more attention. The important thing is to remain in control of your garden. This means choosing plants that work with you, not against you.

It comes back to that old work-versus-enjoyment trade-off again. If the enjoyment returned to you by a plant is worth the effort you put into raising it, go right ahead.

Our totally unscientific and highly personal guide to effort and reward

This isn't meant to frighten you away from certain types of plants, or even from different approaches to your garden. It will, we hope, alert you to the tasks needed to enjoy these plants or garden ideas and help you avoid a crushing workload.

One way to use this guide is to choose the high-maintenance plants you "simply must have," and balance them with enough low-maintenance features to complete your garden environment so that it won't make excessive demands on your time.

Please note: These are strictly our personal reward values. If the sight of a healthy rose garden in bloom sets your heart aflutter like no other experience in gardening, the effort required to care for them will be more than worth it. We've even met people who earn high rewards from the sight of a large, green well-trimmed lawn. Some people like anchovies too . . .

Feature/Plant	Maintenance	Reward
Lawn—Mow every 1 to 2 weeks, fertilize 2 or 3 times a year, trim, weed, water, etc.	High	Low
Vegetable garden—Dig in spring, weed, deal with bugs and diseases, do major clean-up in fall, etc.	High	High
Hedges—Trim several times a year, rake clippings, clean up underneath, etc.	High	Low
Annuals in small containers— Water daily, fertilize regularly, needs special soil mixture, deadhead often (especially petunias, cosmos, etc.)	High	High
Summer bulbs (tubrous begonias, canna lilies, dahlias)—Dig up each fall, store over winter, replant in the spring.	Medium	High

Feature/Plant	Maintenance	Reward
Annuals in large containers—Require same work as annuals in small containers with one exception: they need water every 2 to 3 days rather than daily watering.	Medium	High
Perennial beds—Require spring clean-up, do minimum maintenance during growing season (some staking, cutting back, dividing, deadheading, depending on their needs and plant type).	Low to medium	Very high
Easy-going annuals (salvia, fibrous begonias, dusty miller, etc.)—Fertilize several times during the season, water when necessary, and enjoy!	Low to medium	High
Shrubs and Evergreens—Trim/prune annually.	Low	Medium to high
Ornamental grasses—Cut back in spring, divide every 2 to 3 years.	Low	High
Spring bulbs (tulips, daffodils, crocus, etc.)—Cut off dead flowers and stems and allow the foliage to die down naturally. It isn't necessary to dig up and replant in the fall.	Low	High
Shrub roses ("The Fairy")—Prune lightly to shape or reduce size, if necessary. Cut off spent blooms. Fertilize or add compost in the spring, if you wish (ours don't seem to need it).	Low	High
Hybrid Tea Roses—Fertilize in spring and after first blooming period; prune heavily in spring; deadhead constantly; watch for black spot and other pests and diseases; apply winter mulch protection.	High	High

> ## Excuse us while we have a domestic squabble
>
> *We have a serious disagreement in our family, and since we have failed to solve it over thirty-five years of marriage, it will probably remain a thorn in our collective sides forever.*
>
> *It concerns gladioli. We both love them, but one of us thinks they are worth the effort and the other believes they don't return enough beauty to justify the care they demand.*
>
> *On the one hand, glads are dramatic, colourful and real eye-catchers in the summer. Who cannot resist a bed of gladioli in the sun?*
>
> *On the other hand, they must be removed from the garden, dried and stored in a cool place every fall; the life of their blooms is limited (many gardeners plant groups of them 2 weeks apart after the first frost to create a succession of blooms); they are very fussy about their location (full sun, good drainage); most demand staking to stand upright; and they are susceptible to rot.*
>
> *But hey—if you love glads, go right ahead and plant as many as you wish. One of us will be cheering you on. (No, we won't say which one. All families have their secrets, after all.)*
>
> *—Dave & Cathy*

MAJOR TIME CONSUMER #1: HOW MUCH LAWN DO YOU REALLY NEED?

Lawns are so time-consuming that we've devoted an entire chapter to the subject (see The Lawn As Simon Legree, Chapter Six). Before we get into details about suggestions and alternatives to reduce the burden of caring for your lawn, we want to plant a few thoughts in your mind. Otherwise, many ideas in this chapter may seem either overwhelming or impractical.

One more time: Lawns are wonderful places to play with the dog or toss a ball with the kids, we agree. But a thick green carpet of grass all around your home comes with a major price tag, and we mean more than the time and money you spend cutting, feeding and weeding the grass.

We think most North Americans have far more lawn space than they need, and often more than they can afford, in time and effort, to care for it. The silence of summer weekend mornings in our cities and suburbs is shattered by the growl and buzz of lawn mowers and trimmers. That's one price we pay for lawns. Here's another: Gasoline engines in lawn mowers have been identified as a major source of air pollution, and a single mower can spew out many times more pollutants than a well-tuned automobile.

Before you read further, we suggest you think about all the lawn space you have and ask yourself how much of it you really need. If you have more lawn area than you require, or more than you can care for without cutting into your leisure time, consider reducing it to make way for perennial flowers, native shrubs, evergreen ground covers, ornamental grasses and landscaping materials. Along with saving time and money, you'll help reduce levels of the air and water pollution that are a direct result of too many pampered lawns.

MAJOR TIME CONSUMER #2: CODDLED HEDGES ARE A CURSE

We love shrubs. We don't like hedges.

For generations, suburban gardens were marked by clumps of birch trees and long, neatly clipped privet hedges. Neatly trimmed hedges,

---

A stinging rebuke to hedges

We no longer have high hedges on our property line, but our neighbours have a few. From time to time Dave carries a large stepladder (the hedges are that high!) and a pair of hedge clippers across the garden to give the plants a haircut, on our side at least.

One serious problem with hedges is their attraction to stinging life, including yellow-jackets and hornets. Neither welcomes the arrival of Dave—or anyone else—to trim their household, and the sight of Dave swaying at the top of a ladder, gripping his hedge clippers in one hand and waving off a squadron of yellow-jackets with the other, is both amusing and alarming at the same time.

We have nothing against yellow-jackets and hornets. We just wish they would find homes deep in the woods. If high, thick hedges attract them to our neighbourhood, that's just one more reason to dislike hedges.

—Cathy

---

with corners so crisp you could slice bread on them, are a carryover from formal English gardens. Back then, lords of the manor employed small armies of maintenance people to snip and trim daily, and maintained lawns large enough for polo matches. We don't know about you, but manor lords and polo matches are rare in our neighbourhood these days. We wish hedges were as well.

MAJOR TIME CONSUMER #3: AN OVERABUNDANCE OF ANNUALS

We prefer perennials over annuals for a number of reasons. But we're not totally prejudiced against all annuals; we just feel that many people rely too much on them, creating extra work and spending extra money when a well-established perennial bed can reduce the amount needed to invest in both. People who choose annuals exclusively pay a price for the convenience of "instant" flowers. The price includes:

> • The expense of replacing them each year. A hundred dollars invested in several flats of annuals each spring is lost in autumn; the same amount invested in healthy perennials returns dividends, in the form of new flowers and foliage each spring.
> • The time spent planting. Many people enjoy devoting a long weekend in May to planting their spring annuals. Others can find better— or at least different—things to do.
> • Watering, fertilizing and deadheading. Annuals are sensitive creatures. When they become too thirsty or too hungry, they shrivel and pout, and most need a twice-weekly trim of dead flowers to keep looking their best. Container annuals require daily watering through the summer; take a few days' vacation without arranging for someone to pamper your beauties and you could return home to baskets of dried hay. So while containers are great for splashes of colour here and there, be prepared to pay them attention.
> • Comes frost, and forget 'em. The first good frost of autumn sends most annuals to that Great Compost Pile in the Sky. Healthy perennials may hang around for another month.

But we admit it—pockets of colourful annuals set among shrubs, in hanging containers and patio pots, or as border plants, have a place in our garden. We tend to be selective about them, however. In a Rusty Rake frame of mind, we choose annuals according to these guidelines:

- For instant colour. If you're devoting most of your attention to establishing perennials in one area of the garden and want to avoid a drab appearance in another area, annuals will do the trick. Nothing brightens up a shady corner like a riot of impatiens.
- For containers. We love them set around our patio and hanging from the pergola and other structures. By all means, add container plants to your garden for colour, but don't restrict yourself to them. And to reduce your workload, read some important hints in Chapter Nine first.
- For fillers among new perennials. As the perennials mature and fill out, you'll need fewer annuals between them.

Choosing annuals is often a matter of taste, colour and price. Most annuals are hardy, sun-loving plants resistant to common diseases. Still, try to remember these general suggestions before filling the car trunk with flats of annuals from the nurseries each spring:

- In large areas, mix colours as much as possible. You may love marigolds, but several dozen square feet of orange-coloured blossoms is probably too much of a good thing.
- Consider self-sowing annuals if you intend on filling the same space next year. For most zones in Canada these include forget-me-nots, pansies, some poppies, snapdragons, sweet alyssum, cleome, hollyhocks and calendula. Self-sowing annuals planted in new perennial beds will likely be crowded out in future years as the perennials mature.

Remember that some annuals are more demanding than others. Petunias and marigolds, for example, should be deadheaded regularly. This isn't a difficult chore, but if your time is valuable—and whose isn't?—you may be better off with plants which require little or no deadheading such as salvia and celosia.

MAJOR TIME CONSUMER #4: PERENNIALS THAT NEED PAMPERING

As much as we love perennials, they're a little like family and friends— some are easier to get along with than others. But luckily keeping company with them is a matter of deciding whether they're worth the effort or not.

For example, delphiniums and Annabelle hydrangea (actually a shrub, but treated as a perennial in our Canadian climate) must be staked or tied to show off their beauty. We think they're worth it, so we keep a few in our garden.

Perennials are not labour-free, but some are quite demanding. Our suggestion is this: Start with the less demanding plants; build your garden, your confidence and your knowledge of specific plants; and make your decision about specific plants to include in your garden according to the beauty they bring in return for the care they demand.

MAJOR TIME CONSUMER #5: THE INEVITABLE VEGETABLE

When some people first hear of our garden, their first question is often: "What vegetables do you grow?"

Many people believe a garden is incomplete without vegetables. And we grow a few ourselves, in a far corner.

But year by year, we devote less of our garden—and much less of our gardening time—to vegetables. It's not because we dislike the idea of raising our own food, or the kick of serving veggies that originated in our garden. It's just that vegetables are so darned work-intensive. With very few exceptions—asparagus and rhubarb come to mind—vegetables are generally high-maintenance plants, and we're focusing on low-maintenance gardening here. Later, we'll examine some techniques and ideas to reduce the demands that a vegetable garden places on your time and energy.

The glories of shade

If a good deal of your garden area is in shade, don't be concerned—be thankful! Some of the most interesting plants you can grow in Canada prefer shady areas, and while their blooms may not be as bold as plants for sunny areas, shady plants often have more interesting and colourful foliage. Best of all, many weeds are sun-lovers and don't thrive as well in shade, so the more shade you use, the less concern you may have about weeds.

First, determine the kind of shade you're dealing with:

> • Partial shade is any area receiving sunlight for a minimum amount of time during the day—perhaps less than three hours.
> • Filtered shade refers to the light falling on areas beneath open-branched trees or lattice-work screens. These areas are often called "dappled." There is little or no direct sunlight but the area is bright for most of the day.

- Open shade may be open to the sky, but receives no direct sunlight. The brightness can be high, however, if a good deal of reflected light falls on it.
- Deep shade receives no direct sunlight at all and is usually not open to the sky. You'll find deep shade beneath dense trees, under hedges and very close to the north face of walls and buildings.

Shady areas permit you to plant in layers, the same way nature encourages plants to grow away from direct sunlight. Once again, if you think of your garden as a room (or better yet, as a series of connected rooms), tall trees provide the ceiling; ground cover and suitable perennials create the carpet; and shrubs or small specimen trees become the walls.

Grass won't grow in the deep shade under many trees, and we don't think that's a problem at all. Shade-loving ground cover such as English ivy (*Hedera helix*), Japanese spurge (*Pachysandra terminalis*), lily of the valley (*Convallaria majalis*) or woodland ferns will do just fine in most heavily shaded areas. Or simply apply an attractive year-round mulch such as pine bark or cedar scraps.

Shady areas aren't entirely trouble-free, but you can take a few steps to avoid problems and reduce your chores:

- If the shady area of your garden seems a little gloomy—all dark-green foliage—add some plants with variegated leaves and bright blooms. Many types of hosta, dead nettle (*Lamium maculatum*) and lungwort (*Pulmonaria*) qualify here, and reliable and interesting perennials such as Solomon's seal (*Polygonatum multiflorum*) will do the job as well. For blooms, add bleeding heart (*Dicentra spectabilis*), primrose (*Primula*) and monkshood (*Aconitum napellus*).
- Wonderful effects can be created in shade by blending different foliage, textures and shapes, whether they produce flowers or not. The delicate leaves of astilbe and some ferns, for example, can be spotted among solid and variegated versions of hosta.
- Dampness is both a blessing and a curse in shaded areas. While it reduces the attention you must pay to watering the plants, it can also promote various diseases. It's a good idea to space shade-loving plants a little farther apart than those in the sun to encourage air movement, and make a point of removing dead foliage and debris as soon as you see it.
- Plants set beneath large trees are in stiff competition with them for food and water, so give them an extra feeding of compost or fertilizer from time to time.

Here's where we get into trouble with rose lovers

For many years, saying something negative about roses to gardeners was like standing up in church and declaring you were an atheist. Roses are the focal point of many gardeners, and the site of their prize roses is the first place they take visitors to show off their handiwork.

We understand that. Hybrid tea roses are spectacular and rewarding in so many ways. With large, showy blooms in an amazing range of colours and rich fragrances, most continue to bloom right through the growing season. We're as enraptured as anyone at the sight of a healthy rose bush in full bloom.

Unfortunately, those large, showy blooms come at a price. Most hybrid tea roses are among the most high-maintenance plants of all. They demand pruning, special fertilizer and good winter protection. They are also subject to pests and diseases such as aphids, mildew and black spot. And good roses are expensive to purchase and replace.

Hybrid tea rose fanatics don't care. They're eager to uncover the plants in spring, feed and prune them during the summer, hand-pick aphids and inspect for black spot regularly, then mound the roses and say a few words over them before retiring for the winter.

Our preference is for shrub roses, which are far hardier and less maintenance-intensive than hybrid teas. Look for these names when choosing shrub roses: Fairy, Carpet Rose, Nearly Wild and Country Dancer. We've had good luck with all of them, but the Fairy is outstanding!

Rose breeders are constantly developing strains that resist pests and disease and are extra-hardy to attract gardeners such as us. Two types—David Austin and the Explorer series—promise exceptional performance, although we have not yet included any of them in our garden. You may want to choose them, if roses have a place in your low-maintenance garden.

Not everything in your garden has to grow

If you keep thinking of your garden not as a miniature farm or nursery for plants, but as a personal retreat for you and your friends and family, it can change your entire approach to gardening—and reduce a good deal of maintenance, too.

Make your garden a place of quiet surprises

One of the secrets to creating a successful garden is the use of surprises—coming upon things you don't expect, or that you are not immediately aware of upon entering. Even well-maintained gardens stuffed with healthy, colourful blooms can border on boring if it suddenly confronts you all at once. It's always much more appealing to discover nooks and features as you explore a garden. The "surprises" needn't be extravagant or expensive, and they shouldn't be high maintenance either. Here are a few suggestions you might consider for your project (and by all means, look for "tricks" like these whenever you visit other gardens in search of inspiration):

• Shrubs set in an L-shape to create a corner, masking a bird bath, bench, sundial, statue or rockery from view;

• A lattice-work screen supporting ivy or some other climbing plant, with a carved-stone face peeking at you from between the leaves;

• A water feature—re-circulating in a wall-mounted fountain— that spreads its gurgling sound through the garden from a far corner;

• A garden shed (please—not metal or plastic) sporting its own mini-garden of window boxes or shrubbery;

• Bird houses set on sturdy posts among ground cover or mulch.

Here are some ideas that will not only add a new element of interest to your garden but will also sharply reduce the amount of maintenance needed to keep it ship-shape. They work best in larger gardens, but even smaller city-sized areas can be made more intriguing by adding two or three of the following:

• Add a new patio or expand an existing one. This is, admittedly, an expensive and high-labour project for most people. The advantage, of course, is you need do it just once. A properly installed stone patio needs little more than a periodic sweeping; compare that with a similar area of lawn. An attractive patio also makes it easier to admire and show off your garden. If you enlarge an existing patio, spot it with appropriate, low-maintenance container plants such as geraniums and impatiens (use the New Guinea varieties for sunny areas). Patio tomatoes and a container filled with herbs (dill is a wonderful, easy-growing plant that goes well with almost every summer dish) add interest, flavour and fun to summer meals.

• Add pathways. Instead of separating your flower beds from your house and patio with an expanse of lawn, cut meandering paths across it. Use an old garden hose to trace the route, with several gentle curves. You'll need to remove grass and soil to a depth of perhaps 2 inches; then fill the area with either pea stones or fine gravel alone or combined with flagstones. Paths, by the way, needn't lead anywhere special or even be immediately apparent. We separated a heavy shrub and tree area in a far corner of our garden by making a short path, with random flat-topped stones, leading through it. People—especially young children—love to explore it, following the path to a low-maintenance area set off by a massive landscaping rock. (For The Tale Behind the Rock, see below.)

• Create islands—If you have the space, consider widening your path once or twice and setting an island of perennials in the middle, perhaps dotted with large, interesting rocks. Ornamental grasses and carefree perennials such as salvia (*Salvia superba*), showy stonecrop (*Sedum spectabile*) and lady's mantle (*Alchemilla mollis*) do well in these locations.

• Add another place to sit and relax. There is nothing quite so tempting in a garden as an old bench set beneath a tree, or against a wall, or behind an ivy-covered trellis. Even in a small garden, a nook like this invites you to sit and relax with a good book and a cool drink . . . or with just your thoughts. If you can make use of some item or artifact with a story behind it, you'll add even more interest. A stone bench in our garden, for example, was constructed from a concrete slab that was part of the front porch of Dave's childhood home. He rescued it during renovations to the old house and set it on a pedestal near a lattice screen where our clematis grows. You don't need something this nostalgic, and a bench from a garden supply house will do just fine. But here's a hint: Don't have grass growing under it—you'll waste a lot of time (and maybe slip a disk) reaching under it for trimming and cutting. Set the bench on mulch or gravel instead.

Should you have a water garden?

Water gardens have become fashionable in our area recently, and we admit they intrigue us a good deal. Many of the examples we've seen are

An island in a pathway is an interesting location for ornamental grasses and carefree perennials.

both stunning and restful, especially those with a pump to re-circulate the water and tumble it down a wall of rocks, or spouting water like a fountain in the centre. Fish, turtles, frogs and newts thrive in a balanced water garden, which also attracts dragonflies, butterflies and other fascinating creatures.

Water plants, especially lilies, are beautiful and most water plants are untroubled by pests and diseases. (Some are susceptible to aphids, but one water gardener we know simply sprays them off with a garden hose; they fall into the water, where goldfish gobble 'em up.)

We're intrigued by water gardens, but we're not yet convinced they are a low-maintenance item. If a water garden appeals to you, we wish you luck. And if it proves wildly successful, we may hint at an invitation to visit and "borrow" a few of your own ideas.

The tale behind the rock

Some things in gardening you've "just gotta have." This can lead to more problems than you expect, and can even strain the best of friendships.

In our case, it was a rock. Not an oversized pebble or your average garden-variety stone, but a rock! Dave wanted one for a special place in our garden to fulfil his landscaping scheme. "Wouldn't a large boulder look good right there?" he would say, framing the area with his hands like Steven Spielberg directing a movie. He already had a few shrubs in mind to set around it.

Landscaping boulders aren't all that easy to find in our area. So one day, when Dave heard that two brothers working a farm about a hundred kilometres from us had some landscaping boulders for sale at attractive prices, he had found his source.

The deal was strictly "cash and carry," which meant we would need something larger than our little Plymouth to cart it home. No problem—Dave sweet-talked a co-worker into driving with him to the farm and toting the boulder back in his friend's pickup. It sounded like a pleasant weekend outing, and Dave would pay for gas and coffee along the way. So off they went.

They located the farm, which was dotted with splendid granite boulders, and the two brothers were eager to assist. When Dave finally made his choice—an interesting rock, maybe 3 feet across —the brothers quickly fired up a big front-loading tractor, told our friend where to position the pick-up truck, and went to work.

The rock Dave chose wasn't as large as the iceberg that sank the Titanic, but they both had something in common: most of their mass was beneath the surface. While Dave watched in fascination—and the owner of the pick-up watched in horror— the farmers pried this monster out of the ground, raised it in the air and dropped it onto the bed of the truck, which made a groaning sound and sank to its knees in submission.

Dave, his co-worker, the massive boulder and the traumatized truck travelled slowly back to our home at about 20 kilometres an hour and 4 inches above the roadway. Upon arriving home, Dave recruited every able-bodied person in the neighbourhood, equipped them with shovels and other levers, and rolled the granite mini-mountain off the back of the pick-up. It crashed to the ground, registering about 4.5 on the Richter scale.

I was about to point out that the boulder did not land where Dave had planned to place it, but reality quickly set in and I agreed that it looked just fine right there. Which is where it sits today.

Soon after that experience, we invested in our own pick-up truck. But we've purchased no more landscape boulders.

—Cathy

CHAPTER 4

THE ROOTS OF THE PROBLEM

Many problems encountered by gardeners can be traced back to the condition of their soil. Ideal soil produces healthy plants, and healthy plants tend to take care of themselves. They resist pests and disease better, because some garden insects actually seek out sickly plants to attack, leaving healthy plants alone.

Assessing and changing your soil needn't be as complex as some people expect. True, you can perform spot analyses, sending samples off to a laboratory for detailed scientific examination. But who really does that? Most soils can be improved by following a few simple procedures and keeping in mind a few basic rules, such as:

RULE #1: EVERY SEED WANTS TO GROW

Since every seed wants to grow, it fails only when something prevents it from growing. Soil (and, later, sun) is the source of all life-elements for a seed, and providing reasonable amounts of food, air and water for the seeds is all you need to do when preparing or working your soil. If seeds and seedlings do badly, the problem probably doesn't lie with the seed. The problem is in the soil and location.

RULE #2: A LITTLE WORK ON THE SOIL SAVES A LOT OF WORK ON THE PLANTS

Few people welcome the idea of turning over garden soil with a spade to start a new garden bed—although to us it's a welcome ritual in spring because it means our long winter is finally over.

Good soil preparation can reduce or prevent a lot of problems later by producing larger, healthier plants. And it needn't take a good deal of back-breaking work. As someone pointed out recently, Mother Nature never owned a plough—or a spade, for that matter—yet she never has trouble growing plants. Constant tilling of the soil may not only be unnecessary, it may be unproductive. Starting a new flower bed is usually the only time you should work the soil deeply. (Vegetables are a different matter, of course.) The rest of the time, surface control is more important.

RULE #3: UNDERSTAND THE BASICS

To you, it's just dirt. To the plants in your garden, it's the only home they know.

All soil is made up of five different basic components. Their relative proportions determine the type and quality of soil you have. They include:

> • *Inorganic soil particles.* These determine the texture of your soil and are the result of rock being broken down over millions of years by climatic conditions. Larger rock particles produce sandy soil; medium-sized particles yield silt; and very small particles result in clay.
> • *Organic matter.* This is the nutrient value of your soil, most of it from decomposing plant life. Besides providing food for your plants, organic matter also helps hold moisture in the soil while binding soil particles into granules for air and water to move through the soil.
> • *Air.* Air provides room for roots to extend themselves among the soil particles, and is necessary for continued decomposition of organic matter in the soil.
> • *Water.* Sharing spaces between soil particles with air, water is vital to all life, of course—but it must be in balance. In excessively sandy soils, spaces between the particles are so large that gravity pulls water through them too quickly, and the soil is left dry and arid. Waterlogged soils result in air being forced out from between the particles, suffocating organisms and plant roots.
> • *Soil creatures.* Good soil is teeming with life, all of it essential for the breakdown of organic material into nutrients your plants can use. These little creatures range from earthworms and really ugly centipedes to microorganisms and bacteria. Their presence makes the soil rich and crumbly for plants, and their burrows keep it open to air and water. Generally, the higher the population of these creatures in your

soil, the better its quality. By the way, this is a good reason not to use—or overuse—pesticides, which kill all these little creatures and reduce the quality of your soil.

• *Acidity (pH levels)*. This explanation can be basic or it can be complex. We'll keep it basic. Acid and alkaline levels in soil (measured according to pH levels—neutral is 7; acidic soils measure lower than 7 and alkaline soils measure higher than 7) affect the health of various types of plants. Most evergreens, including rhododendrons and azalea, prefer acidic soil; plants such as purple coneflower, phlox, candytuft, lilac and juniper do well in alkaline soil.

How can you tell which kind of soil you have? You can purchase a soil-testing kit, which is probably a good investment. Here's another idea: collect a couple of tablespoons of crumbled soil in a glass, and add a few drops of cider vinegar. If the vinegar fizzes, your soil is alkaline. If nothing happens, it's either neutral or acidic.

Soil pH can be modified to make it more suitable for certain plants. Adding massive amounts of peat moss (up to half the volume of the soil) makes it more acidic; so will adding sulphur or ferrous sulphite. The addition of pine needles also acidifies the soil, but they require quite a while to decompose. As Rusty Rake gardeners, we prefer to grow plants that suit the existing soil rather than modifying the soil to meet the plant's needs. To make your soil less acidic, add powdered limestone.

RULE #4: ADD A LITTLE KNOWLEDGE ABOUT YOUR GARDEN SOIL

You should have some idea of other soil conditions in your garden, and it doesn't take a complex scientific test to discover them either. Here's what to do (by the way, this is fun to perform with young children, who will think it's cool to play with dirt; they can pick up some science knowledge and maybe even start to believe you're smarter than they thought you were):

1. Place enough topsoil from your garden in a large Mason or pickle jar—about one quart or one litre in size, with clear, straight sides—to fill about a third of the jar.
2. Add water until the jar is almost full.
3. Tighten the lid securely and shake vigorously until all the soil clumps are dissolved and it is evenly mixed.

4. Set the jar on a windowsill and leave it undisturbed overnight while all the ingredients settle.

5. When the contents have settled (if your soil is heavy clay, it may take two or three days to completely stabilize), examine the contents carefully. You should be able to distinguish different layers of soil in the bottom third of the jar. The very lowest layer is sand, marked by distinctive spaces between the granules; mark its height on the jar with a crayon. The next layer is silt; mark its height. On top of the silt is clay, which is the most compact of all levels, revealing no spaces between the granules; use the crayon to note its level. Finally, on top of the clay is organic matter that has settled. Other organic matter may continue to float freely through the water, making it murky. Measure the total depth of the material that settled out, and the depth of all four ingredients—sand, silt, clay and settled organics—then roughly convert them into percentages of the whole.

If the sand layer represents 90 percent or more of the soil profile, your soil is "sandy." Sandy soils drain quickly, but since they have little organic matter they tend to be low on nutrients. What's more, quick drainage tends to wash nutrients from the soil faster. Organic matter in sandy soil decomposes faster, due to all that air between the particles, so compost and other materials must be added more frequently.

If more than 40 percent of the profile is silt, it will drain well, but will still require the addition of organic matter.

If more than 40 percent of the profile is clay, your soil is considered a clay type. It will be more difficult to work, and it drains more slowly. While clay soils usually have high levels of nutrients, these are not easily available to your plants and organic material must be added.

If your soil is a mixture of 40 percent sand, 40 percent silt and 20 percent clay, rejoice—you have loam, the ideal basic soil mixture. It holds moisture, drains well and holds nutrients. All you need is to add organic matter.

RULE #5: THERE ARE ORGANICS AND THERE ARE ORGANICS

Basically, there are four ways of adding organic material to your garden soil. They are compost (everyone's first choice), manure, peat moss and organic bark.

Compost is still the best—and least expensive—way of adding organic material to your garden soil. Do yourself and your garden a favour:

If you don't already have a compost pile in your garden, promise to make one. Now. In fact, put it in writing:

> I promise to start at least one compost pile for my garden, for the environment and for the good of my flowers and my soul, before I plant another flower or trim another shrub.

Sign Here: _____

You can't ignore compost and be a complete gardener

We have become almost religious zealots about compost, so forgive us if we get a bit preachy here.

It's almost impossible to oversell the importance of compost. Compost is one of the few things in life that is pure goodness for both body and soul. For example:

One reasonably sized addition of compost adds as much healthy organic matter to your garden soil as one hundred years of natural decomposition. That's impressive enough, but biologists, botanists, horticulturists and other people with lots of letters after their names tell us that compost can work all these miracles:

- Compost protects plants from pests and disease.
- Compost helps the soil hold air and water, which are essential for plants.
- Compost contains important trace elements, such as zinc, copper and manganese, in the right proportion for plants.
- Soil with adequate levels of compost grows darker, absorbing heat faster in the spring and giving plants a head start on growth.
- Compost releases nutrients to the plants slowly, as they are needed, instead of all at once.
- Compost cannot "burn" plants like some chemical fertilizers.
- By adding vegetable scraps to compost instead of placing them in your garbage, you reduce the total volume of garbage placed in landfill sites.

With benefits like these, anyone who doesn't maintain a compost pile is practically anti-social. And any gardener who doesn't have at least one compost pile is missing out on a major work-saver.

A guide to good composting

In case you haven't yet started your own compost heap, here are the basics:

- It doesn't have to be complicated. You can pay a hundred dollars or more for a sleek plastic composter with bells, whistles and gimmicks. You can also make one out of lumber hammered together into an open-sided box wrapped in chicken wire. Factory-made composters often include animal-proof covers to keep out marauding raccoons, squirrels, possums and rodents. Otherwise, we think simpler is better.
- You may want more than one. Even if your garden is small, you may want two composters—one in a distant corner, behind a shrub or your garden shed, and another near your kitchen door. One is conveniently located to accept dead plants and clippings while you're puttering in the garden; the other is for kitchen scraps, and is handy to your back door during cold winter days. We keep a bucket under the sink, next to the garbage pail, and empty kitchen scraps into the compost every day.
- Try to compost in layers. Composters work best when the material is layered, alternating from grass to plant material or kitchen scraps, then soil and leaves before another layer of grass starts the cycle over again. A layered, well-functioning composter has no noticeable aroma unless it becomes overloaded with one item, such as grass.
- Use no meat or animal products. Besides keeping foraging animals away, it reduces the prospect of aromas even further.
- You can add gimmicks, but . . . Many companies sell aerators, compost-starters and really icky worms to hasten the process. We don't think they're necessary. Composters break material down faster than you may expect, and worms and other little creatures have no trouble locating a well-stocked compost and making themselves right at home.

A colour guide to compost materials

With the exception of discarded flowers and certain kitchen scraps, everything you toss into your compost will be either brown or green. Brown material is dry and rich in carbon; green material is wet and rich in nitrogen. For an ideal mix, try for an equal balance of each. Here are a few guides to the most common items in each colour group:

If the colour is brown, and you're adding:	Be sure to check for:
Fall leaves and dead plants	**Diseased plants.** Avoid adding them; discard in the garbage or try to destroy by burning.
Straw or hay	**Seeds.** They could survive the composting process and sprout where they're not wanted.
Pine needles	**Time.** They take longer to break down than other materials. Use them as a mulch instead, especially under acid-loving plants such as rhododendrons.

The last place you would look

Dave came in from puttering in the garden one day with a familiar request: "Has anyone seen my glasses?"

I looked around the kitchen and in the usual places. Then I asked the usual question: "Where did you have them last?"

The usual response: "On my head. Or in my pocket."

We couldn't find them anywhere. For several days, Dave read his newspaper by holding it at arm's length before giving up and purchasing a new pair.

Time passed with the seasons. Almost two years later, after emptying the bottom of one of the garden composters, Dave trundled a load over to the perennial bed. When he dumped the compost on the bed and began to spread it, the sun glinted off . . . his glasses. They had slipped from his pocket while he had been loading material in the composter almost two years before, and had contentedly settled, inch by inch and week by week, down to the bottom.

Best of all, they appeared unharmed (plastic, glass and metal being notoriously poor compost materials) and with a thorough washing—a very thorough washing—they were back on Dave's ears. Helping him read gardening books.

—Cathy

Twigs	**Size.** If their diameter is larger than your thumb, cut them into small pieces first.
Eggshells	**Nothing.** They're wonderful additions to the compost.
Wood chips	**Type.** Avoid pressure-treated wood chips or sawdust.
Corncobs	**Size.** Some people cut them into short lengths to hasten decomposition. We don't.
Fireplace ashes	**Balance.** Add sparingly and never add ashes from charcoal briquettes used in the barbecue.

If the colour is green, and you're adding:	Be sure to check for:
Fresh leaves or plants	**Nothing**—add 'em all.
Kitchen scraps	**Size.** Peelings and waste from vegetables and fruits are fine. Most vegetable seeds will be destroyed by heat in the compost, so don't worry about them. Every now and then a tomato will make a surprise appearance somewhere in the garden, but it's easy to yank out or even transplant into the vegetable area, if you choose.
Coffee grounds and tea bags	**Nothing.** These rot quickly and are very high in valuable nitrogen. Coffee filters work well, too.
Green grass	**Balance.** Don't overload the composter with grass, and make sure to mix thoroughly with everything else in the pile. Better idea: Use a mulching lawn mower and leave the grass clippings on the lawn.
Weeds	**Seeds.** Put them into the pile before they go to seed.

Flowers	**Nothing**—they're all fine before they go to seed.
Pruned trimmings	**Woodiness.** If they're too woody, chop into smaller lengths.

Excuse us while we clean out the stables

In spite of the benefits of compost, you may wish to add another organic source of nutrients from time to time—specifically, manure. Cattle and horse manure are best, and most easily available. Sheep and poultry manure have higher nitrogen contents, but they may also command a higher price. Stick to horses and cows.

Manure comes in two types: fresh (sometimes called "raw" or "green") and well aged, which means it's at least a year old. For a bunch of reasons, some of them purely aesthetic, well-aged manure is best; green manure may contain unwanted seeds. It can also "burn" plants if applied during the growing season, so if you must use green manure apply it only in the fall. If you are unsure about the age of the manure, add it in reasonable quantities to your compost pile, where it can only do good.

> ### Manure memories
>
> *A neighbour of my mother's believed fervently in fresh pig manure for his garden. Each spring, he would purchase a truckload and spread it thickly among his flower beds, between his shrubs and (gulp!) in his vegetable garden.*
>
> *Unless you have visited, or been in close proximity and downwind from, a pig farm, you have no idea of the impact that fresh pig manure can make on your olfactory senses. For two days, no one on my mother's block could eat, and many of them had trouble breathing. It was disgusting!*
>
> *Finally, the neighbour gave up his practice. Or maybe the smell eventually got to him. I'm not sure. But please don't use green manure—offensive smells and insulted neighbours are not what gardening is all about.*
>
> *—Cathy*

Peat moss and ground bark add some organic qualities to soil, but they make few nutrients available for your plants. Use peat moss to loosen clay soils and add moisture retention for fast-draining sandy soils. Mix it in well, aiming for an even blend of peat moss, clay and compost. Peat moss, by the way, is more effective in a soil mix if it is thoroughly moistened before being blended with the other ingredients.

You can also use peat moss as a mulch, but mix it with compost, well-rotted manure or a decorative mulch first. On its own, peat moss can form a hard crust that's difficult for rain to penetrate.

Speaking of mulches:

Three rules for low-effort gardening: Mulch, mulch, mulch

We love mulches. They save us untold hours of work during the growing season, and we suspect most people don't make enough use of them.

Here's what good mulching does for your garden:

- Insulates the soil, keeping it warmer in winter and cooler in summer. Plants appreciate this kind of comfort as much as you do.
- Minimizes erosion, holding down all that rich topsoil and preventing it from being washed away during heavy summer rains.
- Retains moisture, keeping your beds from drying out too quickly under the hot summer sun.
- Improves the soil and feeds your plants.
- Prevents damage from heaving ground. Hardy perennials can survive cold winter temperatures, but alternate freeze/thaw/freeze cycles will cause the ground to heave, damaging their roots.

All of these are Really Good Things, of course. But from a Rusty Rake point of view, the best of all reasons to use mulch is that it cuts down weeds and reduces the need to till or cultivate the soil. The more you mulch, the less you bend, kneel, stoop and crouch to scoop weeds from your garden and turn over the soil. You also help the environment by spraying fewer herbicides around.

Shredded bark, either pine or cedar, is effective at controlling weeds in a perennial garden and looks attractive as well. But it can be expensive to cover a large area with good-quality bark, even if you purchase it in bulk. Pinewood shavings are cheaper, and they work just as well;

we use them in back areas of the garden where they can't be seen, and we spread more expensive cedar and pine bark and chips up front. We've also "cheated" by applying a layer of inexpensive wood shavings to a depth of an inch or two, and covering it with pricey cedar mulch. It's like putting out our best china for guests.

The mulch is on and the bar is open

We love to entertain in our garden during the summer season. This makes it very much like a room in our home.

But just as you probably vacuum the carpet, pick up the news-papers and dust the furniture before expecting guests, we used to scurry around the garden, cultivating and raking the soil neatly for an hour or so before friends and family arrived.

Mulching solved all of that. It never needs vacuuming, never looks dusty and pleases the eye. Now, before guests arrive, the only thing we're concerned about is having enough ice, drinks and snacks.

This, in our opinion, is Civilized Gardening.

—Dave & Cathy

Whichever mulch you use, don't skimp. Mulches should be 2 to 3 inches deep to be truly effective. Always leave room around the base of your plants—and this includes shrubs and trees—for air to circulate and prevent rot or other damage. Keep mulch an inch or two away from the barks of your trees for the same reason.

Some gardeners fear that slugs and other hungry creatures may hide beneath fragments of bark, but we've never noticed any increase.

Don't forget inorganic mulches such as brick chips, small gravel river stones and volcanic rock. They add no nutrients to the soil, but they're just as good at controlling weeds and they're virtually permanent. Inorganic mulches are especially effective at the base of ornamental shrubs and specimen trees. Spread landscaping cloth, which allows air and water to penetrate but prevents weeds from rooting, on the ground beneath the mulch.

A healthy diet for your plants

Using compost generated from kitchen scraps and garden plants, plus organic mulches, we produce almost all the fertilizer we need for our perennial garden. Only when transplanting do we rely on commercial fertilizers. Then we mix compost with the surrounding soil and add a water-soluble transplant fertilizer that's high in phosphorous. Phosphorous is the middle number in the code that indicates a fertilizer's content. The other two components are nitrogen and potassium. Thus, a 7-7-7 fertilizer has equal (but low—just 7 percent each) quantities of all three.

The ratio of phosphorous is high in transplant fertilizers because phosphorous promotes strong root systems and helps a plant mature faster. (Nitrogen is used by the plant to produce green foliage, so its level is high in lawn fertilizers; potassium aids the production of flowers and fruit, as well as producing strong stems and building resistance to disease.)

Transplant fertilizer is typically 10-52-10, which delivers lots of phosphorous to help the new plant become established.

Many gardeners get into debates about chemical fertilizers versus organic fertilizers. Our position is this: each has its place, but most gardens benefit from organics. They're safe to use, inexpensive to buy, require less frequent applications and contain other nutrients that plants need (sulphur, calcium, magnesium, iron, manganese, zinc, copper) in naturally occurring quantities. Finally, they make sense environmentally by doing what Mother Nature has always done: recycle.

Chemical fertilizers are practical for operators of large farms who (usually) know how to use them safely and sensibly. They're also fine for annuals—especially container plants. While organic farming is growing in size, the prices charged for organically grown fruits and vegetables command a much higher price than those grown by conventional means. As long as farmers can grow their crops more cheaply with chemical fertilizers, and the majority of consumers choose their apples and corn according to price, chemicals will continue to be used by the majority of farmers.

Water-soluble chemical fertilizers are best for annuals because they're easy to apply and provide quick results. Otherwise, we suggest you maximize your use of organic fertilizers wherever possible.

Weeds—when you can't prevent them, control them

Mulching helps control weeds, but it cannot prevent them totally. They always manage to sneak their seeds and roots into places where they don't belong, creating unnecessary work for gardeners like us.

Before you declare war on weeds or even consider surrendering to them, maximize your protection against their sneaky little ways. Mulching is your first defence.

Many weeds can be controlled during spring clean-up. Don't ignore that cute little clover plant in April; within a few weeks its relatives will have migrated everywhere. Pounce on it right away. Weeds are easier to yank out when still young, because they haven't had time to develop a strong root system.

An excessive number of young weeds in your garden may suggest you're using too little mulch. Consider thickening the mulch layer to provide more protection against the weeds.

"It is." "No, it isn't." "Yes, it is." "You really think so?"

Every now and then, our neighbours glance over their fence to see us standing in the garden and pointing at the ground, in serious discussion. Dave often has an open book in his hand. It looks like we're saying a few words over a gravesite—a chilling thought.

Well, we're not.

Dave's book doesn't contain prayers. It contains pictures and descriptions of plants.

This is a Cummins Weed Conference. One of us has spotted a strange green shoot and believes it's a weed and the other has said "No!" because he or she believes it's a new cultivar. We're simply trying to determine whether we should nurture it or kill it.

So if you have ever fed and watered a baby plant that suddenly sprouted into a Godzilla-version of plantain or yanked out a pesky shoot which you later discovered was a struggling dahlia, take comfort: we've all done it at one time or another.

—Dave & Cathy

When the growing season arrives, make daily walkabouts to admire your garden and patrol for weeds. This is much better than setting aside special weeding days once a week, when the task can become overwhelming. It's also more effective after a good rain (wear your boots!), because the plants are easier to yank out of the ground. Every weed you see during your daily walkabout should be immediately yanked and banished to the compost heap—except those that have already gone to seed. The seeds may survive the composting action. Wrap these plants tightly in newspaper and dispose in your garbage or burn them.

Another method to control weeds is by thick, dense plantings. We've seen mature beds of pachysandra, for example, in which a weed has never sprouted, nor is ever likely to sprout. The pachysandra prevents most weed seeds from striking the ground; any seeds that make it through find it dark as a coal mine in the shadow of the pachysandra's leaves.

If weeds seem to be winning a battle, use herbicides only as a last resort. In response to concerns about the environment, chemical companies are making weed-killers less toxic, but the chemicals still represent a risk that can be avoided by home gardeners.

Besides, weeds can be killed with relatively simple methods. Sprinkling common table salt on their foliage can work wonders, for example (but keep it away from any plants you don't wish to kill). So does pouring boiling water on them. This works especially well with established weeds growing through asphalt, paving stones or bricks. We have recently had great luck with common household vinegar, which makes dandelions shrivel and disappear. These are not always instant remedies; they may take a week for full effect. If it hasn't worked after a week, apply again. They're natural, safe and cheap, so they're worth considering.

Pests enjoy your garden more than you do—they eat it

Controlling garden pests comes down to a decision between all-out war and gentle persuasion. We prefer the persuasive route.

All-out war means blanketing your garden with things that kill everything that moves—in other words, chemical pesticides and insecticides. Thankfully, this idea is fading fast, which is good news to everybody including birds, pets, good-guy insects and all of us humans.

The persuasive approach is less dramatic, far safer and more effective in the long run. It means you have to make a few decisions at various stages, but this simply puts you in more control of your garden.

Once again, low maintenance begins with the plants you choose. Some are more susceptible to pests and diseases than others, and by eliminating or reducing the presence of pest-appealing varieties, you automatically reduce your efforts. Highly susceptible plants and their common attackers include:

- Austrian pine (*Pinus nigra*)—diploidia tip blight. This is devastating these trees in our area, and there is no effective treatment.
- Birch—birch leaf miner. The small worms live inside birch leaves, eating the inner cells and turning the tree brown in mid-summer.

• Crab-apple trees—apple scab, rust, fire blight and other problems. Some varieties are resistant to one or more of these pests, but they remain a problem plant.

• Hawthorn—rust and various diseases

• Hostas—slugs. But please don't use this as an excuse to avoid hostas. They're a wonderful plant for shade. In our yard, slugs seem to prefer the white areas of variegated varieties and avoid the thick fleshy-leafed hostas. To battle slugs, stay with the thick fleshy-leafed varieties and avoid too many of the variegated plants.

• Hybrid tea roses—aphids, black spot and mildew

• Iris—borers. Unfortunately, these beautiful plants are easily suscep-tible to wicked little worms that invade and devour the rhizomes—the thick, fleshy root sections of the plant.

• Lupins—aphids.

• Marigolds—slugs and spider mites. Long ago, someone started a rumour that marigolds repel nasty insects and so they should be planted in everyone's gardens. Apparently, two or three varieties actually do serve as natural insect repellents, but we have serious doubts about the practical effect of most.

• Phlox—mildew.

• Zinnias—mildew.

Battle back with tough plants, good bugs and direct attack

Some attractive plants are too tough for pests to bother with, and a few have actually developed a defence against common destructive insects. These are good choices to add to your garden because they're the strong, independent, silent types. They include the rudbeckia family (coneflowers, black-eyed Susans), sedum, day lilies and perennial geraniums, also known as cranesbills. The more you have of these, the fewer demands your garden will place on your time.

Other plants have created a very different defence mechanism: They attract good bugs to (let's not be coy about this) kill and eat the bad bugs. Hey, it really is a jungle out there. The good guys include lady-bugs, lacewings and praying mantises. Ladybugs and lacewings gobble up aphids, mealy bugs, spider mites, scale, thrips and white flies. A praying mantis will eat virtually anything that moves and contains protein—including us, if they were the size of cocker spaniels.

Ladybugs and lacewings will be attracted to your garden by a wide range of plants including most members of the daisy family (such as yarrow, a favourite of ours), tansy and cosmos—especially the White Sensation variety—plus various herbs: dill, parsley, fennel and mint (but be careful with mint; to counter its invasive habits, plant in an open-bottomed plastic container).

Ladybugs and lacewings are also available from commercial sources in quantities of a thousand or so. Don't release them until the cool of a summer evening, however; otherwise, they'll migrate to all your neighbours' yards. The bugs are dehydrated and will be looking for water, so provide moisture from containers of shallow water and pebbles (to allow the little guys to alight on them), or just spray the foliage with a hose.

Don't overlook the benefits of birds in your garden, especially during winter when they're in search of extra protein. Leave berries on shrubs, and seeds on flowers such as rudbeckia, and the birds will visit frequently.

Longfellow got it right

I came across a poem written by Henry Wadsworth Longfellow after he encountered a group of farmers planning to wipe out as many birds as they could. The farmers were convinced that the birds were gobbling great quantities of their seed crops.

Of course, the reverse was about to happen: the insect population would grow so rapidly they would consume far more seeds than the birds could ever eat. It all inspired Longfellow to write:

You call them thieves and pillagers; but know,
They are the winged wardens of your farms,
Who from the cornfields drive the insidious foe,
And from your harvests keep a hundred harms;
Even the blackest of them all, the crow,
Renders good service as your man-at-arms,
Crushing the beetle in his coat of mail,
And crying havoc on the slug and snail.

—Cathy

Here's another trade-off: rudbeckia and other self-sowing plants attract birds during the winter, if you leave their seed heads exposed. Any seeds that the birds fail to eat, however, will produce a crop of new plants in the spring, often in places where they are unwanted. So enjoy the birds in the winter, but be prepared for (perhaps) a little more work in the spring.

Toads are great insect eaters and good company for any garden. If you encounter one, consider setting a "toad abode" in a damp or shady corner. Make it from an inverted broken clay flowerpot, with an entrance for the toad to enter and leave. Unfortunately, toads are indiscriminate in their diets and eat every insect they encounter, both good and bad.

If you have a bird bath, place a stone or two jutting above the surface of the water where beneficial insects can land for a drink now and then. Even better are several shallow containers for insects to drink from. Change the water frequently, or you could be supplying incubators for mosquitoes.

Finally, it's important to practise good housekeeping. Many damaging insects hide among garden trash on the ground. During daily walk-abouts, consign all dead leaves, flowers and other trash to the compost heap.

Bird bath with stones

Toad abode

Hidden Secrets of Plants #1: Tansy

One of the most fascinating things about gardening is the range of different qualities you encounter in plants. Many offer honest-to-goodness medicinal qualities—foxglove, a source for digitalis used in treatment of heart disease, is the best known—but others are less known and even more fascinating. We'll interrupt things from time to time to talk about them. The information may not reduce your gardening workload, but we think you'll find it interesting anyway.

Tansy—the original Latin name was Tanacetum vulgare—was used by the ancient Greeks as a preservative for corpses (we said the information would be interesting, we didn't say it wouldn't be creepy). For centuries, people boiled dried tansy leaves into a liquid that they used to treat intestinal worms, body lice, fleas and garden insects. In small quantities, liquid from the flower heads was used to flavour cakes, cheeses and puddings. Now, there's a multi-talented plant, in our opinion.

From time to time, a direct attack is prescribed. But please be cautious. Too many people reach for a powerful insecticide to massacre destructive insects immediately and in large numbers. Try not to do this for many reasons. Insecticides are like liquid toads—they're indiscriminate in their choice of victims, killing as many good guys as bad guys. Actually, insecticides are much worse than toads because they also affect other garden life, including birds, pets and, if you're not careful, you and your family.

Whatever you do, stay calm

Some gardeners overreact at the sight of a colony of pests. True, watching a herd of aphids suck the juices out of your prize roses is disturbing, even disgusting, but they're rarely fatal to the plant and the situation doesn't need a heavy dose of bug killer. A strong spray from a garden hose will knock aphids off the plant to the ground, where they'll stagger around stunned and confused until something arrives to gobble

We prefer gently curving lines, lending an informal mood to our flower beds. The massed planting virtually eliminates weeds. (Credit: Dave & Cathy Cummins)

Make your garden a joy to explore. This pathway, set between beds of pachysandra and English ivy groundcover, leads nowhere in particular but children—and most adults —can't resist following it.
(Credit: John L. Reynolds)

Another pathway, this time in a sunny area, meanders away from an old stone bench where we sit and admire the flowers in bloom.
(Credit: Dave & Cathy Cummins)

Proving you don't need annuals for mid-summer colour, these are all low-maintenance perennials. Instead of setting plants like soldiers on parade, we mix their heights, shapes and colours. (Credit: Dave & Cathy Cummins)

Our dog Shamus delights in snoozing on this bed of ajuga, set around the base of a tree to cut down our lawn area and protect the tree from our mower. (Credit: Dave & Cathy Cummins)

Wandering pathways, large shade trees and cedar benches all add their own special appeal. Notice the mowing strips separating the gravel path from the grass.
(Credit: Dave & Cathy Cummins)

If a garden has "good bones"—interesting shapes, textures and lines—it will look beautiful through all four seasons. (Credit: Dave & Cathy Cummins)

Everything here shouts "Low maintenance!" The borders, evergreens, trees shrubs and perennials—spotted with annuals for colour—are layered with mulch for weed control. Even the birch tree in the background is low maintenance (it's in our neighbour's yard—a "borrowed view").
(Credit: Dave & Cathy Cummins)

Easter lilies are not supposed to survive Central Canadian winters, but don't tell these beauties set among bee balm (Monarda). They return year after year.
(Credit: Dave & Cathy Cummins)

Shady areas don't have to be all green and mostly dull. The crimson blooms on our astilbe (with hosta in the foreground) almost light up this dark corner!
(Credit: John L. Reynolds)

Start with a basic garden structure like this arbour, hang a container or two from it, and let vines and ivy provide shape and texture. (Credit: John L. Reynolds)

It's often the small details—the unexpected face peeking through the foliage—that make a garden so delightful.

LEFT: (Credit: John L. Reynolds)
BELOW: (Credit: Dave & Cathy Cummins)

them up. For a more gentle but just as effective treatment, drench them with a hand-pump sprayer—the kind used to package window cleaner and dish detergent—filled with a soap-and-water mixture, made with 2 tablespoons of biodegradable soap in 1 litre of water.

In our area, one of the most destructive insects is the Japanese beetle. These bronze-winged bad guys eat almost everything they can land on. Many people try controlling them with traps, but the bait inside the traps will simply attract more of the insects to your garden, so the net result isn't always good, unless you can convince your neighbours to put traps in their yards.

The best advantage you have against Japanese beetles is their visibility. They're easy to spot, usually on the underside of leaves, especially in the afternoon sun. Here are the best ways to deal with Japanese beetles, in descending order of preference:

> 1. *Hand-pick them from your plants.* Wear garden gloves if you prefer, and do it in the early morning—the best time of the day for your garden walkabout—when the beetles' wings are wet and the bugs are naturally sluggish. You can either crush them between your fingers or drop them into a jar of alcohol or a water-and-kerosene mixture. This is especially easy to do when you come upon them while they're doing obscene things right out in the open—you not only scoop two at once, but raise the moral environment of your garden . . .
> 2. *Scoop them into jars.* If you dislike handling creatures this small and ugly, use an empty wide-mouthed jar and cover. Place the jar beneath the leaves where you see the beetles and approach them with the cover. The beetles tend to fly down, directly into the bottle. A few inches of alcohol or a water-and-kerosene mixture in the jar will seal their doom.
> 3. *Invite birds into your garden.* Robins, starlings, cardinals and flickers consider Japanese beetles a delicacy. Attract them with a bird bath. But don't put out birdseed during your beetle battles. Birds are as lazy as the rest of us, and if they can eat at a perch without hunting for flying food, they'll take the easy way every time.

Earwigs are easy to control. These insects are not really very harmful in the garden, but the sight of them makes people uneasy. Instead of spraying insecticide, simply cut an old garden hose into lengths about 2 feet long and lay them at various locations on the ground in your garden. The next morning, fill a pail with hot water and shake the critters out into the water.

Live and let live

One day several years ago, Dave noticed a hornets' nest inside our garden shed. I, of course, insisted that he remove it. Hornets buzzing around my head? I thought gardening was supposed to be relaxing!

Dave, however, assured me that hornets were the victims of bad press. First, they're very beneficial insects because they control pests like cabbage worms. Killing the hornets could also involve spreading dangerous insecticide around. "Besides," he said, "they only sting if they feel threatened."

I asked him to tell the hornets they would not be threatened by me, because I would never enter the shed as long as they were there. And I didn't.

Dave followed a ritual each time he entered the shed. He would whistle as he approached, open the door slowly, wait for the insects to recognize him (I have this image of one hornet calling to the others, "Put your stingers down—it's only Dave!"), and then move slowly but deliberately inside the shed to do what had to be done.

Dave was never stung, the hornets did their thing, and cabbage worms in our garden became as rare as polar bears.

One spring, they were gone. They just disappeared, goin' down the road perhaps to some another garden. Dave almost missed them. Anyway, I had to admit that living with the hornets, instead of blasting them with insecticide, was a better choice all 'round for everyone

—Cathy

The best way to control reasonable quantities of pests such as caterpillars is to hand-pick and drop them into a can or bottle of water with a thin layer of oil or kerosene floating on top. If you spot any eggs on leaves—usually on the underside—remove the leaves and destroy immediately.

Confession time: Even with our best efforts we encounter an overwhelming pest attack periodically, so we resort to pesticides. We choose them only when the pests are seriously damaging a plant or area, and no alternative seems to be working.

If you choose to fight pests this way, please try to follow these rules:

1. Choose organic pesticides over chemical formulas. Organic types use bacteria, viruses, fungi, fatty acids, oils and other ingredients that decompose quickly into harmless, non-toxic materials. Chemical pesticides use ingredients that hang around long enough to work their way through the food chain—from insects to birds and animals, and eventually to you and us.
2. Read the labels carefully and follow the instructions. Don't assume that doubling the concentration doubles the power.
3. Apply them on a dry, calm day.
4. Keep children and pets away.
5. Wear gloves, a long-sleeved shirt and eye protection.
6. Don't allow the pesticide to enter ponds, pools, streams or other bodies of water.
7. Don't apply pesticide to food crops unless the label says it is safe.
8. Wash thoroughly when finished.
9. Store the pesticide according to the label's instructions.
10. Try to be patient; many pesticides take a day or two to do their job.

Do not read this immediately after mixing margaritas in your blender

One day, Cathy returned home and noticed that the blender was half-full of a green, foamy liquid. Perhaps made extra-alert by three decades of marriage to me, she approached no closer.

"What's that green stuff in the blender?" she asked, just as I entered the kitchen from the garden. In my hand was a plastic container of green caterpillars and bugs. The sight of them, and the expression on my face provided the answer almost before I spoke.

"It's, uh, bug killer," I said. "I came across this recipe in one of our gardening books. You collect the pests you're trying to kill and combine them with water and a little liquid soap to make a spray. . ."

"In our blender!" Cathy responded.

Which explained all the green foamy liquid.

The bug spray worked fine.

So did the blender, after its container had been washed, scrubbed, disinfected, polished and washed again, several times over.

—Dave

CHAPTER 5

TOOLS, TIPS AND
TALL TALES

Gardening appeals to people for many reasons, and some Freudian psychologist somewhere can probably dredge up a few dark motives. One of the satisfying reasons we know for tending plants is that it keeps teaching us something new. We can always discover a new type of plant to nurture, a new variety to grow and new ways of doing old, familiar things.

Gardeners also tend to be very sociable. Hermits tend gardens too, we suppose, but we suspect they raise things like horseradish, thistles and thorny roses.

Being sociable, gardeners enjoy chatting and sharing ideas and experiences. So here is our chance to share some thoughts, suggestions and advice we've managed to rake together and store in the garden shed, the one at the back near the rhubarb patch.

Tools you need and
tools you don't

To some people, garden tools are outdoor cousins to kitchen gadgets. These nice people may make melon balls about as often as they shingle their roof, but whenever they see a New and Improved! Automated Melon Baller, they've just got to have it.

We tend to take a more conservative approach.

You need good garden tools, of course, even for a low-maintenance garden. It's just that you don't need as many as you think, and the ones you acquire should be selected according to qualities other than their price, their colour or their appearance in a TV commercial.

We're not golfers, but many of our friends are, and they demonstrate the same passion for hitting a tiny white ball as we have for raising flowers and shrubs. They've taught us a thing or two about choosing garden tools.

Passionate golfers choose their golf clubs according to price, name brand, quality construction and, most of all, the way the clubs "feel" when they are used. The best golf clubs, we are told, will not turn a bad golfer into a Canadian Open champion. But it will make him or her a better golfer than they were before. We suggest you choose garden tools the same way. Better-quality, better-designed tools not only last a lifetime, but actually help you complete some of the more arduous chores in the garden in less time with less effort.

Good tools really are a joy to use. There is something very satisfying about handling a pair of finely crafted pruning shears that aid you in your work by making a precise cut in the perfect location.

Better-quality cutting tools improve the health of your garden. Clean cuts made by good pruners reduce the chance of infection, which can occur in ragged cuts that leave loose bits of plant tissue hanging in the air.

Power tools such as blowers and vacuums are often worth the money... and the noise. We don't have many powered garden tools in our shed—just the ones that save us literally hours of work. And we try not to use them on Sunday mornings. But the ones we invested in, such as the powered vacuum that sucks up leaves and grinds them into mulch, really save us labour.

You may already own most or all of the tools below. But if your current tools don't measure up in quality, or demand too much effort from you—or just, somehow, "don't feel right"—consider replacing them.

SPADES, SPADE-FORKS, EDGERS AND (sorry about this) RAKES

Examine the steel "working end" of these tools. The shovel blades, fork tines and edger should be made of forged steel, like an axe head or hammer head. Cheaper tools are bent and shaped from flat steel like the fender of a car. Forged tools last much longer and tend to do a better job.

Another hint: the longer the socket—the portion extending from the blade to wrap around the handle—the stronger the tool will be.

Handles should be made from good-quality wood such as straight-grained ash or hickory, not pine. The handles on very good spades and garden forks are made by splitting the wood shaft, which means it won't come loose like an attached handle might. Fibreglass and metal tubing also make better handles than cheap wood.

Check for handle length—even a few inches more or less can make a difference to you in comfort and ease of use. Weight is also a factor. Light weight is generally better, but not if it's at the expense of durability.

You may want to have a separate, long-handled shovel for handling compost and manure. Choose one with a sharp, heart-shaped blade.

CULTIVATORS AND LEAF-RAKES

A small three-tine cultivator will be handy to loosen soil around plants. Again, choose a model with forged steel over one with shaped steel. A basic fan rake is best for gathering leaves in the fall. Bamboo is light and attractive, but expect to replace it every two or three years. A quality steel fan rake with spring supports will be a better long-term choice.

TROWELS, HAND CULTIVATORS AND SUCH

Forged trowels and cultivators are preferred over stamped metal, but they don't make quite as much difference here as with spades and forks, since you won't be exerting as much leverage on them. Light weight and handle comfort are more important. But if you choose a pressed-metal shape, ensure that it appears sturdy enough; we've opened some soup cans made of metal more sturdy than the kind used in some cheap bargain-basement trowels.

PRUNING SHEARS, LOPPING SHEARS AND SAWS

You can spend five dollars on one pair of pruning shears and a hundred dollars on another pair. At first glance they will both look similar and even do a similar kind of job. But we think one pair is too cheap and the other is too expensive. Here is what we suggest you look for:

- *Comfort*—Try handling pruning shears as though you were choosing gloves. They should fit comfortably in your palm, and your fingers should meet in the right places.
- *Power*—You don't have to be arthritic to appreciate the benefits of pruners that offer extra leverage. Ask to test a pair before buying,

and choose the one that requires the least effort. Pruning shears should be better at cutting stems and branches than at building hand strength. We have a pair of ratcheted pruners that are lightweight and very powerful. Instead of cutting in one motion, they cut with several small ones. Neither of us have arthritic problems, but anyone who has a problem exerting pressure with their hands would really benefit from this design.

• *Cutting action*—Pruners cut either with a scissors action or an anvil action. Scissors pruners (also known as bypass or "hook-and-blade") work just as the name suggests, with two sharp edges. Anvil pruners use one sharp blade that presses against a flat surface, usually made of plastic or soft metal. Each design has its advantages. To be effective, the scissors blades must be strong enough to withstand sideways pressure during a cut. This means either expensive metal, which raises the price; or thicker steel, which requires more pressure to make the cut. Scissors designs will, however, cut closer to the stem when pruning (but not too close—leave just a little nub).

• *Removable blades*—Well-designed pruners make it relatively easy to remove the blades for sharpening or replacement. You should be able to disassemble the tool for cleaning and lubricating as well. Look for a tool held together with nuts, bolts and locking washers, rather than rivets.

• *Price*—For low-cost pruners, choose the anvil design; cheaply made scissors pruners tend to have problems if the blades are made of cheap, flimsy metal. Good anvil pruners are cheaper to produce. Better-quality scissors designs cost more, but should last significantly longer.

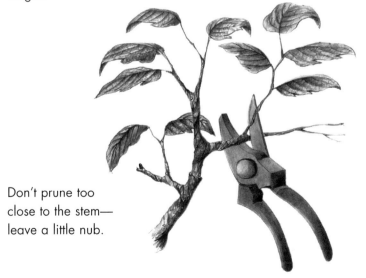

Don't prune too close to the stem— leave a little nub.

It's his story and he's sticking to it

We hope your garden is not infested with Tool Fairies. Because ours is, and they drive Dave crazy.

Mind you, we have never seen one, but we know they must be small, because they can creep into the smallest places—behind the wheelbarrow, for example. They're very clever and cruel, and they must hibernate because they're never around in the winter.

Tool Fairies wait until Dave's back is turned, then they sneak up, steal his pruners, his saw, his clippers or whatever tool he happens to put down—and they hide them in the darndest places! "It was right here a minute ago!" I hear Dave complain. Then he calls the Tool Fairies nasty names and wastes much of the day looking for the tool they have squirrelled away on him.

One day, Dave returned home from the gardening supply store looking smug. "I've got those little rascals beat," he said, displaying something that looked like a canvas corset for someone with a 28-inch waist.

It was a tool apron, designed to hang on the edge of the bucket that Dave carries around for clippings and other materials. Built into the apron were pockets to hold pruners, trowels, forks— every conceivable hand tool in a gardener's arsenal. "They won't get the tools out of here!" he said defiantly. Then he loaded up his new gadget and set off happily into the garden.

You guessed it.

That fall, the bucket vanished—apron, tools and all. We looked behind every shrub, under every bench and in every compost pile. Not a sign of it.

The following spring, while getting the tool shed ready for planting and such, there it was—hidden behind some furniture we had packed away in November. "They're getting smarter," Dave said, shaking his head in wonder.

Stronger too. That bucket and all those tools must have weighed 20 pounds.

—Cathy

Lopping shears provide extra leverage for branches ranging from 1/2 inch to 1 inch thick—too large to handle with pruners, and too small to tackle with a saw. They are also available in scissors or anvil designs, but here the anvil design is preferable because the pressure is so much stronger, thanks to the long handles—usually 24 to 30 inches. Again, wooden handles should be close-grained hickory or ash. Metal or fibreglass handles should come with comfortable, tight-fitting vinyl grips.

Pruning saws can be either hand-style or Swede-style (also known as a bow-frame). Swede saws are larger and a little more awkward, but they're effective on larger branches and limbs, beyond the 3-inch thickness that is the practical limit of most hand saws.

In hand-style pruning saws, beware of double-edged blades, with coarse teeth on one side and fine teeth on the other. You may nick adjoining limbs with the teeth on the opposite side of the blade while trimming a limb.

The key here is easier work, and only a saw blade with set and bevelled teeth will provide it. Before you choose any saw, hold the blade vertically in front of you, facing the teeth. Saws with "set" blades have the teeth bent slightly out at an angle, alternating left and right. Set teeth will make a cut slightly wider than the thickness of the blade, preventing it from binding in the wood. Also, check that the edges of the teeth are bevelled—that is, at least one edge is sharpened at an angle. Cheap saw blades are made by stamping them out of flat metal, with no sharpening at all. With set and bevelled teeth, the saw does most of the work; with flat stamped blades, you do most of the work.

Hidden Secrets of Plants #2: Hollyhocks

In our childhood years, these grew wild in back alleys of the city and alongside old buildings. Now, they're making something of a comeback in old-fashioned flower gardens, although their susceptibility to rust and the die-off of lower leaves in mid-summer can make them unattractive.

The waxy petals of hollyhock flowers were once eaten as a cure for coughs, and the red petals were added to wine to enhance the colour.

SPRINKLERS, SOAKERS, WATERING WANDS AND WATERING CANS

When choosing a lawn sprinkler, try to avoid the back-and-forth models that gently spray water into the air. Much of the water from these models actually evaporates before it settles on the ground; swing-and-shoot reciprocating designs are more effective.

Best of all are soaker hoses, made of plastic or canvas, that seep water directly into the soil. They're not practical for lawns, but they're ideal for flower beds and vegetable gardens. Here's a work-saving hint: Lay your soaker hoses down in early spring before the plants have had a chance to produce much growth.

Watering cans range from a few dollars in price to (we're not kidding) a couple of hundred dollars. The latter are made in Britain, sport excess brass trim, and are used for either watering the geraniums at Buckingham Palace or making tea for the Queen.

Cheap watering cans are plastic and can do the job. Better watering cans are metal, tend to have longer, narrower spouts and do the job a little better, with more class. Take your pick, but you may want to invest in two different sizes for convenience.

Watering wands are wonderful for extending your reach and providing regular drinks of water to hanging container plants or those set behind flower beds. They're lightweight and inexpensive, and produce a gentle flow that won't damage delicate shoots or seedlings.

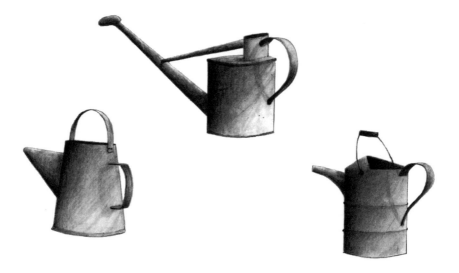

Watering cans with long spouts (top) extend your reach, are very attractive—and usually more expensive. We get by with inexpensive designs.

Finally, think about rain barrels. These were standard items for our gardening grandparents, and the current generation is discovering their benefits all over again. Some rain-barrel fans swear that plants grow healthier from its natural chemical-free qualities. Well, perhaps. But there's no doubt that rainwater collected in barrels and spread on flower beds can sharply reduce the water consumption of many communities. Modern rain barrels also include screens to keep mosquitoes from using it as a nursery for their young. A rain barrel is one of those gardening ideas that means a little more work for you, we admit. In return, you can feel good about your contribution to environmental protection.

WHEELBARROWS AND CARTS

These are essentials for moving plants, trucking tools and carrying compost, fertilizer, mulches and the like. Sturdy metal barrows with inflatable rubber tires and long wooden handles look great and last a lifetime, but we've seen some clever new plastic units that are easier to handle and much cheaper. Once again, choose for comfort and buy the best you can afford.

TOOLS FOR COMFORT

Gardening gloves, of course. Our favourites are cotton gloves with a roughened rubber coating on the palms and fingers, available from popular work-clothing stores. The cotton is comfortable, and the rubber coating keeps your hands dry. Add rubber boots or clogs, a wide-brimmed hat and perhaps a heavy apron with pockets to hold tools. Most of all, a kneeling pad.

NEAT EDGES AND STURDY SUPPORTS

These aren't technically tools, but they'll save you scads of time and work.

Black plastic edging, which sits in the ground so only the rounded upper edge is visible, adds a neat appearance and reduces trimming time in the garden. If possible, choose the heavier-gauge landscaping grade, available from building supply dealers, for maximum appearance and longer life. We still prefer flat stones or bricks over plastic edging, but they admittedly take more time and effort to install.

Wire supports for peonies, hydrangeas and other plants are great, but don't wait until the plants are falling over to install them. It's far easier

> ### Two "garden gimmicks" that really work
>
> *Every year, someone introduces a new gimmick that promises to save work for gardeners. Sometimes they do, but usually they don't. We've discovered two items that really have saved us time and effort, and recommend them to Rusty Rake fans. (No, we don't get a commission from each sale, and we're not even sure who the manufacturers are.)*
>
> *The first is the Bucket Apron, a canvas "skirt" that hangs from a metal or plastic bucket and holds pruners, knives, twist-ties and other small tools. It's wonderful for daily walkabouts and puttering, and it's more difficult to misplace a bucket than a pair of pruners—although this has happened from time to time . . .*
>
> *The other is one I appreciate because of back problems. It's called a kneeler stool. When I want to sit, it's a comfortable seat; when I want to kneel, it's a cushion for my knees, and the legs provide leverage to help me stand up again. So if you suffer from the Tool Fairy problem, or your back doesn't enjoy gardening as much as you do, consider adding these to your tool arsenal.*
>
> *—Cathy*

to position these in early spring and allow the plants to grow into them rather than installing the supports or cages around a plant in full flower.

And there's a better alternative to tomato cages, in our opinion. When the plants are heavy with fruit, the cages and plants can fall over too easily. We prefer new spiral stakes, which tend to be much more steady and dependable.

You can add other tools if you wish, such as long-reach watering cans. Enjoy! But we suggest you start with the best-quality basic tools you can afford. After that, everything else is mostly fashion.

What about tools you don't need? A gas-powered tiller is fine for turning over new beds, but you're much further ahead to rent this equipment. And we don't trust any garden tool that is "not available in stores" and is sold only through TV commercials.

Good ideas for gardening we've begged, borrowed, stolen and even discovered ourselves

We love hearing about ingenious ideas to make tending our garden easier. Here are a few we've collected over the years:

> • *Stash tools in handy places throughout the garden.* Instead of finding a reason not to tie back that drooping plant or prune that shrub when you pass it during a walkabout, store inexpensive small tools and twist-ties in a metal rural mailbox set on a cedar post at the back of the garden. Decorate it with a bright design, or camouflage it in brown paint. It will keep tools and such handy for quick on-the-spot fix-its that can save hours of work down the road.
>
> • *Extend your reach.* As a safer alternative to climbing ladders when pruning tall shrubs, trees or ivy, extend the handles of your clippers with inexpensive plastic tubing—the kind used by plumbers for drains. Purchase a 6-foot length, choosing an inside diameter that just accommodates your clipper handles; cut it in half and force-fit the clipper handles inside the two lengths. Now you have clippers with sturdy, lightweight handle extensions to reach high without a ladder.
>
> • *Widen your paths.* If you have narrow pathways across your lawn, consider widening them for easy access . . . and less lawn.
>
> • *Identify your plants.* Even we get confused now and then about the plants in our garden, especially in spring when everything looks young and green. ("Is that a primula over there in the corner . . .?") Metal stakes with label areas you can write upon—the same kind

Label your plants with their full name and source to avoid confusion . . . and impress visitors with your professionalism.

used in nurseries and public gardens—identify the plants for you and your guests. More important, you can add other details such as the date they were planted and their origin. It's easier than keeping it in a book . . . or in your head.

• *Spread your gardening across the year.* It's natural to stop thinking about your garden after frost has set in and all the plants are mere skeletons of their former selves. Don't wait until spring, for example, to review last year's failures and successes. Make a note of them in autumn, or whenever the thought is fresh in your mind ("I will never try to grow delphiniums again—ever!") rather than waiting for spring ("Maybe some delphiniums would look like nice against the fence...").

• *Add a camera and a notebook to your roster of gardening tools.* Take photographs of your garden from time to time during the growing season, then use the photographs to remind you of plants you want to relocate, remove or replace the following spring. (They also help you show off your successes to friends who may miss your garden at its prime.)

• *Start a garden notebook and carry it with you when you visit other gardens in search of ideas and inspiration.* It's often difficult to remember the Latin terms for interesting plants, so write them in your book and add little sketches here and there when you see a grouping or landscaping feature that appeals to you. (Don't worry about not being a Michelangelo—you're the only one who needs to understand them.)

• *Save straight branches of varying lengths when pruning shrubs and trees.* They make perfect stakes to support plants that need assistance in standing straight and erect.

• *Use a heavy plastic sheet when pruning.* When doing a major pruning—usually in the spring—pull the tarp or sheet with you as you move around the garden. Place branches on the sheet, so you can easily bring it with you to the compost heap, truck or other location for disposal. It's much easier than walking around picking up twigs and branches later.

It's a bird! It's a plane!
No, it's a low-flying wheelbarrow!

When our children were tykes, the neighbourhood was heavily populated with other young children, and our yard was still mostly flat, open and grassy. One weekend a year, for several years running, the children would find ways to raise money for charities by selling baked goods, washing cars, staging backyard talent shows, and so on. It was all very sweet and very middle-class suburban.

One year, our son and daughter asked their father if he had any ideas for a fundraising event. They wanted something original, "something nobody else in the neighbourhood has done before!"

That kind of challenge was enough to kickstart Dave's imagination into action. He spent the evening in his basement workshop, and emerged the next morning with two plywood panels, a large fan blade and some paint. Then he attacked our garden wheelbarrow.

Within a few hours, our wheelbarrow had been transformed into a green airplane complete with wings, spinning propeller and a clean "cockpit" normally used to transport grass clippings.

Word spread among local children like wildfire: For 5¢, a mere nickel, you could take a "flight" around our backyard in an open-cockpit airplane complete with propeller and engine noises from the pilot—who, of course, was Dave, pushing from behind.

Soon our driveway looked like the entrance to a ride at Disneyland. All day long, children stood in line clutching nickels, waiting for their "flight" around our backyard. Many took multiple journeys, dropping their nickels into the jar, taking their flight, then scurrying around to line up again.

The ride was so popular, it almost killed Dave.

You see, the only way to spin the propeller was for Dave to run at full tilt around our yard (remember—it's a third of an acre) pushing the "airplane" and its passenger ahead of him, "banking" the craft on turns and flying low under our trellis before taxiing back to the driveway/landing strip again. By the fifteenth or so passenger, he had to stop for refuelling, but Cummins Air was committed to all-day service. By the end of the day, Dave felt as though he had flown south with the geese, migrating to South Carolina.

Dave survived, the charity prospered, and the kids had something to talk about all winter long.

The wheelbarrow was never quite the same again, however.

Next year, our kids asked Dave if he had any suggestions on raising money for the charity again.

He suggested a lemonade stand.

—Cathy

CHAPTER 6

THE LAWN AS
SIMON LEGREE

Green lawns are wonderful places for picnics, for playing golf and croquet, and for kicking a soccer ball around with your grandchildren. They're attractive to look at as well, although the pleasure received in admiring a lawn is in direct proportion to the depth of its green colour.

We love the sight, the feel and the smell of a healthy green lawn as much as anybody. We just don't believe it's worth all the effort, beyond a certain point.

High prices are paid to maintain those vast, green manicured spaces spread around our city and suburban houses. The city of Victoria, British Columbia, discovered that only about 2 percent of all the water it collected, filtered, treated and pumped to residences was actually used for drinking and cooking. About a third of the rest was scattered over lawns—and Victoria is hardly a city with a drought problem.

Damage is done in many different ways. Gasoline lawn mowers are notorious sources of air pollution, adding to the smog problem in large cities, and the run-off of lawn fertilizer eventually finds its way into our water supply, promoting the growth of algae and other water-pollution problems. Many of these problems, we suspect, are caused not just by homeowners but by contracted lawn-care organizations whose trucks rumble through neighbourhoods spraying mysterious liquid nutrients and pesticides on lawns. We're not suggesting that these firms are careless with their chemicals, or that all the operators are poorly trained and indiscriminate. We're just concerned that it's so unnecessary. Does it give you a feeling of security when you're out for a stroll, for example, and you encounter a sign on a neighbour's lawn warning you to stay away because it has just been sprayed with a poisonous substance? Organic-based fertilizers are safer than pure chemical formulas and, in the long run, they're more effective.

Consider the problem of grubs in your lawn. These larvae of June beetles infest lawns on a seven-year cycle. But if their major damage occurs only in a year or two out of the cycle, why spray every year?

There is no natural benefit to raising countless acres of thick green lawns. Grass doesn't naturally grow in an unbroken expanse trimmed less than 2 inches high and watered through the dry summer season.

For most people, their lawn is the space they walk across to get to their flower beds. It's rarely a source of enjoyment; but it's frequently a source of constant work, from April to October.

We may, in fact, be the last generation of North Americans to worship The Almighty Lawn in its present form. Recent years have seen a groundswell of support for the idea of smaller lawns generally and, for city dwellers, no lawn at all in the front of their houses. Many urban residents have replaced their front lawns with mulch, ground cover, gravel, brickwork, stones, flower beds, or a combination of them. They often look great, and they demand a small percentage of the effort needed to maintain a pristine lawn. Smaller gardens, front or back, don't need a lawn of any size to be successful, and a postage-stamp lawn in a courtyard garden simply looks, in our opinion, silly.

So before getting into low-maintenance lawn care—which many people consider an oxymoron—start be reassessing your entire approach to the green slave-driver that does nothing but lie around your house.

> • *Reduce the size of your lawn.* This may be a revolutionary idea for many people, but think about it long enough and you'll get used to it.
> • *Identify the low-use areas of your lawn.* This is the first place to look when following suggestion #1. If your lawn includes areas that you never walk upon except to feed, cut and water the grass, they're probably the first to eliminate.
> • *Replace grass in low-use areas with low-maintenance, sun-loving shrubs and small evergreens such as Spirea bumalda 'Gold Mound' and Bird's Nest Spruce (Picea abies 'Nidiformis').* Also, consider adding hardy evergreen ground covers, or clumps of ornamental grasses set among mulch.

• *Are wildflowers the answer?* Some city dwellers have begun a "return to nature" movement by digging up their lawn surface and scattering the seeds of native wildflowers over the soil. This may be a little over the top, in our opinion. Many native wildflowers, rightly or not, are referred to by a nasty word that begins with "W" and rhymes with "seeds." An idea that's hatched in good faith eventually looks like an adventure in chaos. We think "low-maintenance" and "neatness" are not necessarily conflicting concepts. We also like to stay on good terms with our neighbours, who may view a wildflower meadow in our front yard with deep suspicion and disturbing hay-fever symptoms.

• *Discover the beauty of ground cover.* Some ground-cover plants are so low maintenance, attractive and interesting that we're amazed they aren't used in place of high-maintenance grass. An expanse of ground cover, the right size and in the right place, adds an entirely new dimension to your garden. We find it much more relaxing to look at than the pool-table surface of a closely mown lawn. Most ground covers also tend to be drought-resistant with vigorous root systems. Long after lawns have turned brown in summer heat, healthy ground cover remains lush and green. There's more: many thrive in shade, which defeats most grasses, and on sloped areas a thick ground cover is the very best protection against erosion. We give the entire topic more attention below; read on.

• *Stop mowing hillsides.* If your lawn includes a slope, why are you trying to grow grass on it? Mowing a grassy slope is a difficult, futile job—and an unnecessary one. Our suggestion: rent a culti-vator, dig up the soil, rake off the grass roots, and plant a thick perennial ground cover such as periwinkle or pachysandra for shady areas. If the slope receives full sun, choose cotoneaster, day lilies or low-growing junipers. Your mowing, watering and feeding days on that particular part of your property are over—and we bet the appearance will be enhanced, especially during long hot spells of summer.

• *Eliminate trimming.* After mowing, many gardeners spend extra time with a string-trimmer or similar tool, trimming the edges of their lawns where the mower cannot reach because the grass grows against a fence or wall. Why? Install mowing strips at ground level. Use bricks, gravel, railroad ties or similar materials to separate the lawn from the structure, and your trimming days are over. Mowing strips made of bricks or flat stones are also useful in separating grass from flower beds.

Caring for the Big Green Slave-Driver

Unless you're a courtyard gardener, you will probably always have some lawn area to care for. So let's review a few time-and-effort savers before we move on to serious alternatives.

- *Don't overfeed the lawn.* Excessive applications, especially of high-nitrogen quick-release fertilizer, actually weaken the lawn by stimulating blade growth at the expense of root development. Twice-yearly feedings, in spring and fall, with an organic slow-release fertilizer will produce a healthier lawn and less work for you. By the way: the fall feeding is the most important.
- *Practise good watering habits.* Of all the errors gardeners make with their lawns, most are associated with watering. Usually it's watering too little and too frequently, which is the best way we know to promote weed growth in your lawn. The average lawn needs about an inch of water per week during the growing season, either from rain or from your sprinkler. Practise good watering habits this way:
  — Invest in a swing/reciprocating sprinkler that shoots a good stream of water across the lawn, not one that sends a delicate spray into the air. A surprising amount of water from fine-spray sprinklers quickly evaporates into the air.
  — When you water the lawn, make it one good watering per week if necessary. Set a small plastic container beneath the sprinkler and continue the flow until an inch of water has been collected.
  — Don't water in the hot afternoon sun, when most of the water will evaporate. Best time of all: early in the morning, just at sun-up. Second best: In the evening when the sun is low. (This is the only practical time for many people who are rushing off to work or other destinations every morning.)
- *In the dog days of summer, why water at all?* Grass naturally goes dormant during dry spells—always has, always will. Blades turn brown, and roots snooze. This does not, we admit, produce an attractive appearance. You can overcome this with heavier watering, but your municipality may place restrictions on such activity. So unless you're spending most of your time on—or staring at—your front lawn, why not leave it *au naturelle*, as it were? Normal lawns will recover quite nicely with the arrival of autumn rains. Society just has to get over this idea that a brown lawn in summer is a sign of failure. It is not—it's a sign of grass plants going through a perfectly normal stage of life. You may want to water the lawn in your back garden more

often; it probably deserves more attention because that's where you may be spending most of your time.

• *Give some thought to when and how you mow.* Avoid cutting the lawn when it's still wet after a rain—it's far too difficult. Don't cut your lawn too short. We suggest maintaining a minimum height of about 2 inches all year round. One exception: your final cut of the season, before snow arrives, should be somewhat shorter. This will prevent snow from compacting and smothering the grass blades.

• *Invest in a mulching mower—with a grass-catcher.* The best thing to do with grass clippings is grind them into fine mulch and leave them on the lawn. True, grass clippings are fine additions to your compost, but too much grass will upset the compost balance, slow decomposition—and smell terrible. Mulching mowers work well when grass is dry and when you're not mowing more than once a week. But in spring and fall, when grass grows faster (and is often damp), mulching mowers lose their effectiveness. Instead of healthy mulch, your lawn acquires a dangerous build-up of thatch. Try attaching a grass catcher to your mulching mower every second cut, and transfer the clippings to your compost pile.

A virtually carefree carpet for your outdoor living room

We confess: Without extensive use of ground cover, our garden would be almost too much to handle.

Ground-cover plants are among the best friends in our garden. They're virtually maintenance-free, they add interesting tones and textures to the garden, most are pest-resistant, the thickest of them crowd out weeds, and we mix-and-match them for new effects from time to time.

The single most-important step you can make in cutting work time in your garden is to replace appropriate sections of lawn and annual beds with an attractive mix of perennial ground cover, especially around trees, beneath shrubs and in the shade.

There. We said it and we're glad.

So here's our guide to ground cover. Please give it serious consideration. These plants are wonderful additions to any garden—interesting, reliable and soothing to see. Just follow a few suggestions:

• *Don't limit yourself.* Periwinkle, pachysandra and hosta are all fine ground covers, but your choice is much wider than these three. It's restricted only by soil type, whether the location is in shade or sun, and how much (or how little) you want the plants to spread. Sweet woodruff (*Galium odoratum*), for example, makes a fine ground cover in open shade. In the sun, consider fleeceflower (*Polygonum affine*) and low-growing junipers. Choose from perennials, herbs, shrubs or vines.

• *Mix for a change of texture and colour.* We planted ajuga among ground-hugging juniper, just because we felt like it. Both plants get along fine together, with the smooth-leafed dark-toned ajuga poking slightly above the rough-edged juniper branches.

• *Give it some thought.* More than any other plants in your garden, except trees and shrubs, ground cover should be considered semi-permanent. Once many ground-cover plants make themselves at home, they become very difficult to evict. Mark your site, consider its exposure to sun, check the soil (is it sandy or clay? in direct sun or shaded all day? does it drain well?) and the effect you want to achieve —flowering plants or green foliage? A smooth layer or different textures? Evergreen or herbaceous?

• *Prepare the soil.* This is work, we admit, but a little extra effort at this stage eliminates problems down the road. The most important con-cern here is the elimination of any resident perennial grasses and their underground stems. Once that's done, add generous quantities of compost, peat moss and manure, mix well, and you're on your way.

• *Be patient.* If you have limited time and unlimited money, you could have professional landscapers install a mat of ground cover immedi-ately. But if you're like the rest of us, you'll want to position the new plants carefully and let them grow together into a tight grouping. This may take two or three years to achieve. In the meantime, light appli-cations of mulch between the plants will reduce weeding and improve appearance until the ground cover fills in the spaces.

Below is our guide to favourite ground covers. It's not complete by any means, but it includes plants we enjoy because of their attractive appearance and low-maintenance qualities.

Name	Height	Qualities	Maintenance
Carpet Bugle, Bugleweed (*Ajuga reptans*)	10 inches (in bloom) 2 to 4 inches at other times	Spreads quickly in sun or shade. Spikes of blue flowers in late spring. You can walk on it—our dog, Shamus, loves to sleep on a bed of ajuga.	Shear off spent flowers in early summer (use mower at highest setting).

Name	Height	Qualities	Maintenance
Cotoneaster (*C. horizontalis, C. dammeri*)	12 to 18 inches	Full sun or partial shade. Forms a glossy green carpet; its white spring flowers turn into red berries that last through winter. This fast-growing plant is very good on banks and slopes.	Prune annually if necessary.
Cranesbill (*Geranium macrorrhizum*)	12 to 15 inches	With fragrant leaves and pink flowers from spring to early summer, this is a pretty favourite for sunny or partly shady locations.	Deadhead to prolong flowering.
Day lily (*Hemerocallis*)	18 to 36 inches	Different varieties can ensure blooms through most of the season. Does well in any soil.	Remove spent flowers. Divide every 3–5 years.
English ivy (*Hedera helix*)	6 to 8 inches	Dark lustrous foliage. Forms a dense cover in shade or part sun. (May need protection from winter sun)	None.
Fleeceflower (*Polygonum affine*)	6 to 12 inches	Another easy-care plant that does well in almost any type of soil. In summer it sports pink or red flower-spikes resembling bottle brushes.	None.
Goutweed (*Aegopodium podagraria* 'Variegatum')	12 inches	The good news: It will grow almost anywhere. The bad news: It will grow almost anywhere. Control its invasive qualities with a permanent barrier such as a driveway or sidewalk.	Cut off the flowers if you don't like the the look of them.

✓ Front

Name	Height	Qualities	Maintenance
Japanese spurge (*Pachysandra terminalis*)	8 inches	Excellent evergreen cover for shade or partial shade. Spreads by underground stems; forms a tight mat. Creamy white flowers in spring. Slow to establish, but worth the wait.	None. During first few years, prune after flowering to increase spread.
Junipers (*Juniperus horizontalis*)	12 inches	Light-green to steel-blue colour. Adaptable to most soil types. Full sun.	None.
Lily-of-the-valley (*Convallaria majalis*)	6 to 10 inches	Sweet-scented white flowers in spring. They prefer part- to full-shade in almost any kind of soil —moist or dry, rich or poor—forming a lush mat of green foliage.	May need to control spread.
Mother of thyme (*Thymus serpyllum*)	10 inches when blooming	Small aromatic leaves and very prostrate habit make it excellent for use around walks and on hot sandy slopes. Tiny, rosy/lilac flowers in summer. Full sun.	None.
Periwinkle (*Vinca major; V. minor*)	18 inches for major, 8 inches for minor	Trailing evergreens with purple, blue or white flowers and dark-green foliage. Prefers shade, but tolerates some sun (and flowers better). Well-drained soil.	None.
Spotted Dead Nettle (*Lamium maculatum*)	6 to 8 inches	Does very well in shade. Prefers moist conditions, with white or pink flowers in the spring. Two varieties—Beacon Silver and White Nancy —have silvery foliage.	None.

(handwritten marginal notes: "√ Front" beside Junipers row; "√ Front +" beside Mother of thyme row)

Name	Height	Qualities	Maintenance
Plantain lily (*Hosta*)	Wide range, depending on variety.	Everyone's favourite for shady areas. Mix foliage colours for extra interest (but a large area of just one variety can be sensational!)	Watch for slug damage, especially on white areas of variegated varieties.
Goldmoss stonecrop (*Sedum acre*)	2 to 3 inches	Spreads by creeping, forms mat of leaves with tiny yellow flowers from spring to mid-summer. Good for dry soil and rocky areas.	None.
Dragon's blood stonecrop (*Sedum spurium*)	6 inches	Thick mat of rounded, red-tinted foliage with showy red clusters in summer. Dry soil and rocky areas.	None.
Sweet woodruff (*Galium odoratum*)	6 to 8 inches	Lance-shaped leaves with white, star-shaped, scented flowers in late spring. Prefers shade and moist conditions—add humus to soil if necessary.	Clean up old foliage in spring.
Winter creeper (*Euonymus fortunei*)	12 to 24 inches	Evergreen trailing vine up to 36 inches long. Uniform leaves and rapid growth.	Trim back with pruners to maintain desired height.

side ✓

Grasses we love

In the past few years gardeners everywhere—including ourselves—have begun to discover ornamental grasses, and their appearance in gardens everywhere is something we applaud and you should consider.

Ornamental grasses have about as much in common with the grass on your lawn as grape juice has with champagne—their origins are similar, but everything else is different. They add dramatic shapes to any garden and are especially attractive when backlit by the sun, so try planting

Hidden Secrets of Plants #3: St. John's Wort

Between religion and medicine, this attractive little shrub has quite a reputation for such an unassuming plant.

During the Middle Ages, St. John's wort (Hypericum prolificum) was believed to repel the devil, and was a popular ingredient in exorcisms. At least part of the legend was based on the plant's leaf markings, which medieval folk believed resembled the wounds on Christ's palms and feet. Thus, the Knights of St. John's used the leaves as dressings to heal the wounds of Crusaders— but it didn't work.

The plant normally blooms around June 24th, which happens to be St. John the Baptist Day, thus inspiring its name. Medicinally, it has been used as a sedative and as an anti-inflammatory treatment. That's the good news. The bad news: some people are highly allergic to the plant, and rubbing against it may create a severe allergic reaction.

But we like it anyway. Just handle with care and a little respect.

some taller versions at the east or west perimeters of your garden where the rays of the rising and setting sun can show them off.

Tall ornamental grasses have a special place in new suburban developments. They provide much-needed backyard privacy when you can't afford a fence and are still waiting for shrubs to grow.

All shapes, all sizes, almost no maintenance

Don't assume that all ornamental grasses boast long, slender green blades. Some billow like fountains, others stand tall and proud; you can choose grasses that have textures ranging from smooth to stiff to saw-edged, with plumes like rabbit tails, ostrich feathers or silken threads. Many are multi-coloured and variegated in shades of blue, red, white and yellow. Sedge grass has a lovely mahogany tone all year round. The grass clumps even look great in winter, swaying in the wind and, when snow arrives, creating interesting white sculptures.

But here's the best part:

Few plants in your garden will require less maintenance than a mature planting of ornamental grasses. Plant them in almost any kind of soil, match their light needs to the location's sun and shade exposure, water well the first year, and leave 'em be. Besides being virtually maintenance-free, grasses look attractive on their own and as a setting for more spectacular flowering plants.

There's a message in here, and it's this:

We think anyone with a garden, whether they're concerned about low-maintenance ideas or not, should have a few ornamental grasses somewhere—or their garden is simply incomplete.

Ornamental grasses, available in a wide range of sizes, textures and even colours, add new interest to any garden—and most are virtually maintenance-free.

Now that we've taken such a firm stand on the idea, here are some ways to get the most enjoyment with the least work from your ornamental grasses:

> • Mix various sizes, shapes and colours either in clumps of grasses set among mulch and rocks or amid showy perennials such as purple coneflowers or black-eyed Susans.
> • Taller grasses should be placed in the centre of clumps or as a backdrop for blooming plants.

• For edging plants choose shorter grasses, such as Elijah Blue (*Festuca glauca*) and purple moor grass (*Molinia caerulea* 'Variegata').

• Take care with fast-spreaders. While most ornamental grasses remain in their original clump, others have a habit of becoming invasive by sending out underground shoots. The result is too much of a good thing, which translates into Not Such A Good Thing. Common grasses that can become invasive include ribbon grass (*Phalaris arundinacea* 'Picta') and blue lyme grass (*Elymus arenarius* 'Glaucus'). Fortunately, there's an easy solution: Before planting any of these or other invasive plants in your garden, place them in large plastic pots with the bottom removed. Then plant the pot. The walls of the pot will prevent underground "runners" from spreading, and the plant will be able to obtain sufficient nutrients and provide good drainage.

• Don't pamper them. Very few ornamental grasses require heavy doses of fertilizer. Some, if fed too much, may actually suffer by producing soft, unmanageable growth. Better to risk underfeeding than overfeeding.

• They're tardy. Most are slow to get started in the spring. Don't despair—watch for fresh green shoots after most perennials have already begun growing again. When new shoots are established, cut back the previous year's growth.

• If clumps become too large, or if foliage in the centre of the plant begins to die, it's time to divide the plant. Do it in early spring. Separate gently into smaller clumps and plant in other areas of your garden. Or trade a few for other types from a friend who also has ornamental grasses.

• Learn (or at least write down) the Latin names. So many types of ornamental grasses exist that the common names become confusing. It's best to identify the qualities you're looking for, write down the Latin names, and take the list with you to a garden centre with a large collection of these plants. Some plant nurseries specialize in ornamental grasses. Phone around to find one in your area that offers the widest choice.

Your handy guide to great grasses

The following is a guide to commonly available perennial grasses that do well in most Canadian climate zones. Each season, new varieties appear, but these are tried-and-true and are excellent places to begin.

Match the conditions or plant qualities to your needs, plant almost anytime of the year—and enjoy!

Name	Height	Qualities
Blue fescue (*Festuca glauca*)	12 to 18 inches	Sun or light shade. A good accent or edging plant in beds. We especially like 'Elijah Blue'. Stays in a clump. If you don't like the look of their seed heads (we don't), cut them off.
Blue lyme grass (*Elymus arenarius* 'Glaucus')	24 to 30 inches	Bright blue arching leaves, wider than other blues. Spreads well, but dies down in winter and can be invasive.
Blue oat grass (*Helictotrichon sempervirens*)	18 to 24 inches	Sun or partial shade. A good feature plant and the best of the small grasses, in our opinion. Remains in a clump all through winter.
Feather reed grass (*Calamagrostis* x *acutiflora* 'Karl Foerster')	4 to 6 feet	Pink flower heads turn to tan in summer. Narrow dried acutiflora flowers are very effective all summer and winter—wonderful when blowing in the wind. (We saw this on a garden tour and immediately wanted to rush out and buy some.)
Fountain grass (*Pennisetum alopecuroides*)	3 feet	Full sun. Has arching form with feathery plumes in August and September. Needs winter protection in cold climates.
Japanese blood grass (*Imperata cylindrica* 'Rubra')	16 to 20 inches	Sun or light shade. Flat green leaves turn red. Needs winter mulching in cold climates, especially during its first year.
Sarabande silver grass (*Miscanthus sinensis* 'Sarabande')	4 to 5 feet	Full sun. Plumes appear in late August or September. Wonderful in winter when the sun shines on the plumes; withstands snow and wind.
Pampas grass (*Cortaderia selloana*)	6 to 9 feet	A fantastic showy grass with plumes like ostrich feathers. Unfortunately, it thrives as a perennial only in parts of British Columbia—in other zones, treat as an annual.

Name	Height	Qualities
Red fountain grass	3 feet	Full sun. Pink to purple plumes.

(*Pennisetum setaceum* 'Rubrum')		Often grown as an annual.
Purple moor grass (*Molinea caerulea* 'Variegata')	1 to 2 feet	Sun, partial shade. Very attractive, with green and yellow-striped foliage. Purple flower spikes in August.
Ribbon grass (*Phalaris arundinacea* 'Picta')	3 feet	Has attractive white-striped leaves. Be warned—it's a notorious spreader, difficult to remove once established.
Switch grass (*Panicum virgatum* 'Squaw')	4 to 5 feet	Sun, partial shade. Very graceful. Has narrow green foliage with delicate reddish-purple flower heads in August-September.
Variegated maiden grass (*Miscanthus sinensis* 'Morning Light')	4 to 5 feet	Full sun. Has slender leaves with white margins, giving a silvery effect—the entire plant seems to glow when backlit by the sun (hence the name).
Zebra grass (*Miscanthus sinensis* 'Zebrinus')	4 to 6 feet	Sun or partial shade. Green and yellow cross-banded leaves. Good specimen plant.

Fairy rings, lawn artillery and spacemen

Thirty years ago, when we purchased our house, the backyard was an unbroken expanse of poorly maintained grass. We did our best to maintain the rear lawn, but it never looked very good.

One day Dave came inside and said, "The lawn is cursed!" He led me outside and showed me strange markings that had begun as dark green rings but were now brown circles of dead grass. "They're fairy rings," he said, adding almost convincingly: "We've got evil spirits here, dancing in circles at night and killing our lawn."

Not quite true, of course. As a lawn expert told us, fairy rings are caused by fungi that settle in when a lawn needs de-thatching. He advised Dave to rent a de-thatching machine, a special device that would rip out the layer of dead material (the "thatch").

A build-up of more than half an inch of thatch weakens the plants and leads to problems from pests, diseases and the fungus that causes fairy rings.

Dave dutifully rented a de-thatching machine, which turned out to be a mechanical monster that looked like an army tank on the end of a handle. In a warning tone, the rental dealer suggested Dave wear protection when walking behind the de-thatcher. "They kick up a lot of stuff," the man said. "Stones, twigs and things. Put something on to protect your eyes, and it might be a good idea to wear something on your arms and chest as well."

Dave took the warning seriously. After unloading the de-thatcher from a truck, he disappeared into the basement and emerged an hour later, looking like something from a really bad space-aliens movie.

Along with safety glasses and a hat, he had donned heavy cardboard cut to fit over his body and around his arms and legs. It all gave him the gait and appearance of Frankenstein's monster after several strong drinks. Watching him as he walked stiff-legged behind this big, noisy machine, being bombarded by rocks and clumps of dirt, I didn't know whether to fall down laughing or rush out and hug him.

Anyway, he finished the job at great cost to our bank account and Dave's self-esteem, leaving our lawn looking like the surface of the moon. It never recovered. We finally gave up and installed a new lawn. This marks the beginning of our disenchantment with lawns generally, and our interest in low-maintenance plants.

We captured it all on our 8-millimetre movie camera. If Steven Spielberg ever decides to make a really tacky space movie of alien robots destroying the earth, we've got a great comic scene for him.

—Cathy

CHAPTER 7

RUGGED INDIVIDUALISTS
IN YOUR GARDEN

Some people's heroes are their parents, or a favourite aunt or uncle, a special teacher, a brave dog or even (for people our age) an actor like John Wayne.

We have heroes too. But many of ours are plants.

Heroic plants have the same qualities as heroic people. They're independent, trustworthy, brave and reliable. They ask for no special treatment, but they are always there when you need them. Some of our plants are like that, so why shouldn't they be heroes? (We admit it: no plant to our knowledge has ever jumped in deep water to save someone from drowning, but we're trying to make a point here about reducing your gardening chores.)

Most of the rugged individualists in our garden are shrubs and small trees. While annuals and perennial flowers provide colour, the shrubs and trees give our garden shape. Without them, our garden would have colour without form, like a nicely painted unfurnished room. A combination of mature shrubs and specimen trees surrounded by ground cover is a delight to our eyes and our backs—they require an hour or so of attention each spring, a brief inspection during our walkabouts each day, and not much more for the rest of the year. On snowy winter days, they provide interesting bones to our garden, continuing to lend it shape, form and texture.

Trees and shrubs also add privacy and banish unwanted views of near or distant structures. Plus, they are perfect for awkward places—that far corner of the garden, perhaps, or the lost area between your garden shed and a perennial bed.

Mind you, we have the advantage (?) of a large lot, permitting us to space several shrubs in ideal locations and attractive groupings. We have also enjoyed the benefits of caring for the same garden area for over thirty years, providing both the space and time to experiment with several varieties of shrubs and ornamental trees. Our proximity to the Royal Botanical Gardens, and the volunteer work we perform there, has given us a good deal of exposure to different tree and shrub types over the years—experience we want to share with you.

Spacing and selection make a major difference

Most people love the sight of a healthy shrub as much as we do, especially when it's in full flower. Unfortunately, many shrubs are neither chosen nor planted to take advantage of their best qualities.

True, many shrubs make nice hedges. But who needs hedges that require pruning? Attractive shrubs should be given an opportunity to show off a little. But please don't make the mistake of spacing your shrubs in an expanse of lawn, dropping them sparsely here and there like candles on a birthday cake. In fact, we suggest you don't plant shrubs anywhere on your lawn without at least separating them from the grass with a wide "moat" of ground cover. This way, you'll avoid the time and trouble of trying to mow the lawn up to and under your shrubs. More important, you'll protect the shrub from damage caused by striking its trunk and lower stems with the lawn mower,

Like candles on
a birthday cake—
that's how some gardeners
plant shrubs and trees.

Grouping shrubs and trees, with perennial ground cover around them, is more attractive to the eye and requires less maintenance.

scraping off bark and opening the plant to possible insect infestation or disease.

Many landscape architects propose planting the same variety of shrubs in large groups around a property—a setting of junipers over here, a gang of spirea over there—because it suits their sense of design. This is fine for some people, but we're plant lovers and we especially like a mix of "characters" in our garden. Besides, by carefully selecting and locating shrubs according to their blooming times and foliage, you can always have one or more of them at their peak all through the growing season and even beyond, if you include species that produce colourful berries that remain in place in winter, adding colour and attracting birds.

Our insistence on a variety of shrubs, we confess, has created a few problems in the past. Like you, we have succumbed to the allure of a beautiful flowering shrub we simply "must have" in our garden—only to discover later that we are dealing not with a Rugged Individualist but a Prima Donna. Prima Donnas are like some movie stars whom you love to see on the screen but you may prefer them living in Hollywood instead of your spare bedroom.

We've been most successful with small shrubs by placing them against a fence line, combined with evergreens and ground cover. Larger shrubs serve as borders to lend privacy or define a line in our garden, separating a quiet corner from a riot of blooming perennials.

Ideas for selecting shrub locations and types

We've said it before, but it bears repeating here: Don't select your plant before you select its home. This is even more important with shrubs than with most perennials. A Japanese maple that flounders in the wrong location is more than a disappointment—it could represent the loss of a few hundred dollars. Most nurseries offer a one-year guarantee on their more expensive stock, but some shrubs may struggle for a year or more before giving up the ghost. So prior to setting off for your garden centre, determine where you want the shrub placed and choose a plant suitable for that location.

Here are some guidelines:

> • *Evaluate the usual—sun/shade, dry/moist, acidic/alkaline.* Make a judgement call here, based on suggestions from earlier chapters. You may desperately want a rhododendron, but if the location you've chosen for it has sandy, alkaline soil, is exposed to prevailing winter winds, and receives a full day's ration of direct sun, you're condemning the plant to a certain death.
>
> • *Look into the future.* The shrubs and ornamental trees you choose are children, many of whom can be expected to grow into adults— tall, brawny adults that could dwarf you and your house. Many gardeners make the serious error of placing a cute little shrub against a wall of their home, and ten years later both they and their house are living in the shadow of an unjolly green giant. We know one instance in which a gardener planted a row of rhododendrons (again!) next to the exterior of a house with picture windows overlooking an attractive ravine. Later owners of the house lost their view when the plants had grown to roof-height. Not only that, but the rhododendrons grew at an angle away from the wall, extending themselves so far that their roots were unable to hold them firmly in the ground and they literally fell to their deaths. This all took twenty-five years or more, of course, but it demonstrates the problem nevertheless.
>
> • *Consider posture.* Some shrubs stand straight, others slouch. Both have a place, but consider the impact of their appearance on your eye. Upright shrubs with a pyramid shape appear formally rigid, while slouchers are relaxed and laid-back. An upright plant standing amid shrubs that mound, weep or spread horizontally is pleasing to the eye.
>
> • *Mix colours and textures.* Leaves are at least as important as blooms on a shrub because you'll be looking at them longer.

Try mixing foliage colours such as burgundy, gold, blue-grey and shades of green. Combine leaf shapes and textures as well, and you'll create a more interesting visual effect than a monotone of colours and shapes.

• *Mix blooming times.* Even in an average-sized garden, it's possible to have at least one shrub in bloom from April through September. As you add flowering shrubs, try to select new plants that will be in bloom when the others are not.

• *Be choosy about your shrubs.* Once again, many shrubs and ornamental trees can represent an investment of a hundred dollars or more. For that price, you have a right to be choosy about the health and overall quality of your purchase. Look for nicely shaped plants, with several strong shoots rather than a single branch shooting skyward. Avoid any plant with dead leaves at the bottom or foliage that is either yellowed or drooping.

• *Prepare the site.* Again, the usual: Make a hole slightly larger and deeper than the root ball of the plant, and add compost and peat moss to the soil already there. (This is important. If you replace all the soil with a rich mixture of compost and peat moss alone, the roots may not develop sufficiently in search of nutrition.) Ideally, blend one third of each of the materials—local soil, compost and peat moss. Place a layer of this mixture in the bottom of the hole, just enough to lift the plant to the same height as it grew in its original location. Keep some transplant fertilizer handy for an initial feeding.

• *Disturb the roots as little as possible.* If the root ball is wrapped in burlap—a common practice with larger plants—there's no need to remove the burlap entirely. Unfasten it from around the stem or trunk, keeping it beneath the root ball when you set the plant in place. The plant's roots will grow nicely around and through the burlap and you reduce the risk of root damage. For plants in containers, slice the bottom of the container away and check the compactness of soil around the roots. If it's well compacted, slip the blade of a long knife around the inside perimeter of the container, turn upside down, and gently remove the plant and root ball. If the soil is loose, it's best to make long, vertical slits in the sides of the container, place the plant and container in the prepared site, and cut or slide out the remains of the container walls. This should cause minimal disturbance to the roots. If you see a mass of tangled roots with hardly any soil, the plant is probably root-bound. Help it get started by gently separating the root mass as much as possible.

Mixing sizes, textures, colours and postures of shrubs and ornamentals creates an eye-pleasing arrangement. Bonus: There's little room and less light for weeds to sprout beneath them.

> • *Water well at the beginning and keep watering through the first year.* Good quantities of water will help settle large air pockets around the plant and stimulate root development. It's especially important to ensure the plant is watered sufficiently just before winter sets in. After its first winter, the plant should be able to locate its own water, if conditions are right.

Favourite low-maintenance shrubs and ornamentals

Much of the joy of gardening comes from growing plants that are a little out of the ordinary and that also deliver large quantities of satisfaction for minimum measures of effort.

Here are some interesting characters we've enjoyed in our garden, and we suggest you consider for your own. Most are available from larger nurseries. In place of zones, we've indicated hardiness; your garden nursery operator should give you some good advice about the suitability of any plant below for your area. (Remember that, depending on location, many plants can do well in less temperate zones than expected. A location near a heated building, sheltered from direct winds, can assist a less-hardy plant through a tough winter).

Dave & Cathy's All-Time Favourite
Low-Care Shrub List

Name	Description	Qualities
Annabelle hydrangea (*Hydrangea arborescens*)	Ours dominates the garden when in full bloom. We treat it as a herbaceous perennial in our area. Prune back to lower new buds in spring, when growth begins. Huge white globe-shaped flowers appear year after year (15 years and counting for ours!) Only problem: It may need staking to keep the heavy blooms off the ground.	No serious pests in our experience even though some books claim it's subject to various problems. Partial shade and rich, well-drained, moist soil. Up to 3 to 5 feet high.
Beauty bush (*Kolkwitzia amabilis*)	Fabulous pink and yellow flowers appear in June. This shrub grows in a fountain shape and is breathtaking when in full bloom. If you try to prune it, the plant will shoot off in all sorts of strange directions.	No serious pests. 6 to 10 feet high. Full sun with room for growth.
Blue-mist shrub (*Caryopteris x clandonensis*)	Perfect for adding colour in the fall, with lovely blue/violet flowers. Foliage is an interesting grey-green colour. Ideal for small gardens and courtyards. Prune back in spring to new shoots appearing at the base —flowers appear on new growth.	No serious pests. About 2 feet high. Full sun and well-drained soil.
Burning bush (*Euonymus alatas*)	The plant gets its name from its flaming-red foliage in fall. Use almost anywhere—as border shrub, in groups, to screen unwanted views or as a specimen plant. Although some books advise well-drained soil, it has thrived in the clay soil in our garden.	No serious pests. Up to 10 feet high. Sun or shade.
Butterfly bush (*Buddleia davidii*)	Succulent, caned, arching shrub, flowering in mid-summer. Plant in groups or in a perennial border. Prune to new shoots at base in spring. Available in a variety of colours.	No serious pests. 5 to10 feet high. Full sun.

Back

Name	Description	Qualities
Doublefile viburnum (*Viburnum plicatum* var. *tomentosum*)	This large shrub is very elegant, with large white blooms in early summer. Reasonably hardy, but not for northern areas. Its horizontal lines are a nice contrast to vertical plants. Choose loose, well-drained soil. (All viburnums are beautiful shrubs; this is a personal favourite of ours. Not for small gardens, but when in bloom it's a showy delight.)	No serious pests. 10 feet high with a 10-foot spread. Full sun.
Summersweet clethra (*Clethra alnifolia*)	White, fragrant flowers appear in summer. Good for a border; does well in wet areas. Highly attractive to bees. Hardy for most zones.	No serious pests 3 to 8 feet high. Shade.
Siberian pea-shrub (*Caragana arborescens* 'Pendula')	Among the hardiest of all shrubs in Canada. A weeping form grafted to a standard pea-shrub stem, with bright yellow flowers appearing in summer. Tolerates poor soil, drought and winds (the larger standard version is used as a windbreak in Saskatchewan). The thread-leaf variety is especially attractive for such a tough plant.	No serious pests. About 4 to 5 feet high. Full sun.
St. Johns wort (*Hypericum prolificum*)	Has bright yellow buttercup-like flowers, about 1 inch, in mid-summer. Works well in a border or as a mass planting. Attracts bees when in bloom. Slow grower.	No serious pests. 1 to 4 feet high. Full sun or partial shade.
Vernal witchhazel (*Hamamelis vernalis*)	Flowers very early in the spring, before the leaves form. On cold days, the flowers roll up to avoid freezing, extending the flowering period to 3 to 4 weeks. In fall, the foliage turns bright yellow. Its dense growth makes it fine for screens and unpruned hedges.	No serious pests. 6 to 10 feet high. Sun or partial shade.
Virginia sweetspire (*Itea virginica*)	A very pretty shrub. White flowers appear in the spring. Leaves turn crimson in fall, and can be spectacular. Best-suited for temperate areas. Prefers moist soil.	No serious pests 3 to 5 feet high Sun or shade.

And now the runners-up

The shrubs listed above have two qualities important to us that are probably meaningful to you as well. They are attractive, and they require minimum attention and maintenance.

But we can't ignore a few others that have a place in our garden and perhaps can earn a place in yours as well. More common and less maintenance-free than those listed above, these Honourable Mentions are still worth considering. Just be prepared to visit them a little more often for grooming, inspections and general discipline:

CORKSCREW HAZEL (*Corylus avellana 'Contorta'*)

Also known as a "Harry Lauder's Walking Stick," this is a difficult specimen plant to resist. Its branches twist and curl in a convoluted manner, with large rough-textured green leaves that appear to be withering. In winter, its twisted branches are fascinating, especially when dusted with fresh snow. But in our area, they have become a favourite of Japanese beetles and other leaf-chewing pests who rarely kill the plant but leave the foliage looking ragged. An attractive feature plant in a garden, but be prepared to go beetle-picking in summer.

DAPHNE (*Daphne x burkwoodii*)

A low-growing evergreen plant, this is a beautiful flowering shrub suited for patios, courtyards and rock gardens. Oceans of exceptionally fragrant rose-pink flowers appear in early summer and sometimes a second blooming occurs later in the season. Unfortunately, it's a little temperamental (qualifying it for our Prima Donnas list) and somewhat short-lived in our climate—winter protection is a must. Also, watch for leaf spots, canker, aphids, mealy bugs and scale.

DWARF SPIREA (*Spiraea x bumalda* cultivars: Gold Flame, Gold Mound or Dakota Gold Charm)

These are attractive, low (2 to 4 feet high) shrubs, ideal for courtyards and small gardens, or as a "filler" plant in larger gardens. Their foliage is a lovely gold colour in early spring and again in fall. Tiny flowers, pale to deep pink, bloom in large clusters in late May or June. Spirea in general are susceptible to problems, but the dwarf varieties are more resistant and make great little garden plants. (We have experienced no problems with ours—it's one of the toughest plants in our garden.) Trim them back severely in the spring to get beautiful bright new foliage. After flowering, a "haircut" trim will produce a second foliage—lighter than the first but still worth having for a little effort.

ROSE-OF-SHARON (*Hibiscus syriacus*)

In our part of the country, you can't drive very far in late summer before encountering a Rose-of-Sharon in full bloom. We have one in a very protected spot in our own garden. They're attractive, but a severely cold winter can create dieback, especially if the plant isn't protected from the wind. Although many gardening manuals suggest it's a target of various pests and diseases, we haven't noticed any unusual problems.

A primer on pruning

Many gardeners fall into extreme positions when it comes to pruning their favourite shrubs. They're either overly cautious or out of control.

Cautious pruners nip and snip here and there, doing little more than tidying up the plant. At the other extreme, some gardeners attack their plant like lumberjacks, as though they were more interested in producing a cord of firewood than helping a plant look its best.

One of the most important decisions is choosing when to prune. Most plants should be pruned in early spring, at the end of their dormant season.

Give flowering shrubs a little more thought before attacking them with clippers. In most cases, spring bloomers should be pruned immediately after flowering; summer bloomers should be left until the following spring, just as new growth begins.

Here are our suggestions for pruning shrubs:

- Start with any dead, diseased or broken branches—remove them entirely.
- Look for any branches rubbing against each other, and remove all but one of them. The abrasions can open a wound on the plant, leading to infection.
- Avoid simply shearing the top of the plant. To thin it, remove one or two of the oldest stems or canes growing out of the base of the plant. Your goal is to admit light into the middle, encouraging new growth in this area.

- To reduce a shrub's height, trim the longest or most awkward-looking stems by up to one third.
- When looking for a place to prune, choose a location just above an outward-facing bud.
- When pruning evergreens in spring, start by removing winter kill, then prune lightly for shape and to keep the plant dense.
- Unless you're into topiary—carving plants into shapes and sculptures—strive for a natural look that is neither flat-topped nor smoothly rounded.

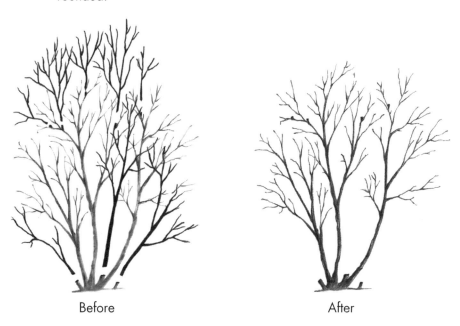

Before   After

Just in case something goes wrong . . .

Our favourite shrubs are attractive and low maintenance, but they're not perfect. If troubles arise with these plants, they're generally due to some basic problem you should be able to identify from the list below.

If you notice an overall decline in the plant:

1. Confirm that you've chosen the correct site.
   - Is it receiving enough sun? Perhaps too much?
   - Did you water it well in the first year?
   - Is the soil type correct—sandy, loam or clay?
   - Does the plant need acidic soil (most evergreens do) or less acidic conditions?
   - Does the plant require more protection from wind?

2. Did you plant the shrub at the correct depth? Most shrubs should be planted with the soil level just above the crown—the point on the stem where the roots begin. Planting too deeply encourages rot to set in at the base of the plant; planting the roots at a shallow depth will cause it to heave in winter, damaging the root system.

3. Are pests or diseases attacking the plant?

4. Was it root-bound when you planted it? Did you ensure the root ball was broken up a little?

5. Are its "feet getting wet?" Try a location with well-drained soil.

If no blooms have appeared:

1. Give it time. Some shrubs require a season or two before becoming established enough to produce blooms.

2. Did you prune at the correct time? (See page 108 for pruning tips.)

3. Fertilizer with a nitrogen content that was too high may have been applied.

4. Frost may have nipped the buds while they were forming.

5. The plant may be attacked by pests or disease.

Vines and ivy for arbours and pergolas

Garden structures provide an opportunity to add a vertical dimension, and we love 'em. They also act as important "bones" to your garden, giving it shape and interest in the winter season.

Many low-maintenance perennials are available to dress up your garden structures. Remember that some vines and many ivies can be aggressive growers, so you may have to cut them back from time to time during the growing season. Don't let this deter you, however. A thick, healthy climbing plant in full flower is breathtaking!

Our favourites, for their combination of eye-pleasing appearance and few demands on your time, include:

CLEMATIS

Choosing a clematis is either great fun or great frustration, because so many varieties exist—large and small flowers, early and late bloomers, and of course a wide range of colours. Remember that all clematis plants prefer morning sun and like to keep their feet cool, so introduce some ground-cover plants or mulch around the base of the plant.

We especially love 'Nelly Moser' (white flowers with pink bars—but avoid hot, sunny locations) and 'Ernest Markham', which has an exceptionally long blooming time.

Note: When purchasing any clematis, be sure to ask the nursery about its pruning requirements. Pruning time for clematis depends on flowering time and whether new buds set on old wood or on the current year's wood. There are many groups of clematis, and cutting back at the wrong time can be disastrous for flower production. A good nursery will provide the information you need.

CLIMBING HONEYSUCKLE (*Lonicera x brownii* 'Dropmore Scarlet')

The hardiest of the twining honeysuckle vines for Canadian gardens. The long-blooming trumpet-shaped flowers are often followed by red berries. Free of serious pests and diseases.

Side Lattice

CLIMBING HYDRANGEA (*Hydrangea anomala subsp. petiolaris*)

Lovely, virtually maintenance-free climbing vine for partial shade—a north- or east-facing wall is ideal. In summer, you'll be presented with a profusion of perfect white flowers. They take a little time to feel at home, however; give them two or three seasons to establish themselves.

FIVE-LEAF AKEBIA (*Akebia quinata*)

A twining grower with attractive dark bluish-green foliage. It flowers in May with fragrant, unique brownish-purple blooms.

KIWI VINE (*Actinidia kolomikta*)

This twining vine grows 15 to 20 feet or more, with showy variegated foliage. White, fragrant flowers appear in May and June.

SILVERLACE VINE (*Polygonum aubertii*)

A vigorous, rapid-growing twining vine with good foliage. It grows under most conditions; white flowers appear on the upper parts of its branches in late summer.

Evergreens—The blooming bones of your winter garden

The term "evergreen" includes a wide range of plants, even though most people immediately think of pine trees, junipers and cedars. It consists of every plant that retains its foliage through the winter (and even some that don't), including broadleaf evergreens such as euonymus, boxwood and rhododendrons.

In the bleak days of January, your evergreens often play the role of the only (apparent) living thing in your garden. So be sure to select and plant some evergreens for their visual appeal and their low-maintenance qualities. Here are some suggestions:

- *Mix the shapes and colours.* Unless you're seeking a totally formal effect or building a thick hedge wall, don't line your evergreens up like soldiers—all the same size and shape. Evergreens look best when grouped in threes, mixing flat-leafed plants such as boxwoods and rhododendrons with needled plants.
- *Do the natural thing.* Most evergreens look best when allowed to assume a natural shape.
- *Consider slow-growers and dwarf varieties.* You'll reduce the pruning and avoid problems with oversized plants later.
- *Purchase carefully.* Quality evergreens are a good investment in your garden, but they're not bargain plants. Choose only healthy evergreens with burlap-wrapped balled roots, or plants in containers.
- *Use good timing.* Needle-leafed evergreens should be planted only in warm soil, so wait until the leaves are on the deciduous trees in the spring, or when the leaves have begun to turn in the fall. This gives the tree time to develop its roots. Water well, especially during the first year.

In the spirit of Rusty Rake Gardening, here's our guide for trustworthy low-maintenance evergreens. Try to find room for two or three in your garden.

Name	Description	Qualities
Large Specimens		
Nootka false cypress (*Chamaecyparis nootkatensis* 'Pendula')	A very attractive pendulous form. (We happen to like pendulous or "weeping" varieties; other people think the plants look sick.)	Few problems. Grows about 25 feet in 20 years. Full sun.
Serbian spruce (*Picea omorika*)	Has excellent foliage and doesn't grow as wide as blue spruce.	Few problems. Grows to 60 feet after 50 years. Likes partial shade.
White fir (*Abies concolour*)	Slow to medium grower	Few diseases or insects, but dislikes heavy clay. Grows 30 to 50 feet. Full or part sun.
Smaller Specimens		
Bird's nest spruce (*Picea abies* 'Nidiformis')	Dense, spreading, slow-growing shrub with a hollow "nest" in centre.	5 feet after many years. Partial shade.
Mugo pine (*Pinus mugo*)	A low-growing, spreading shrub —choose a dwarf cultivar such as 'compacta' or 'var. pumilio.' When "candles" (new growth) appear each year, reduce them by half to control height.	Grows to 2 to 5 feet for dwarf varieties; standard varieties from 10 to 15 feet. Sun and light shade.
Winter creeper euonymus (*Euonymus fortunei*)	We favour two cultivars especially: 'Emerald Gaiety' with white margins on deep green leaves that acquire a pink tinge in winter, and 'Sun Spot', a round compact form whose green leaves have yellow centres. These broad-leaf evergreens can be used as ground cover or as small shrubs in mass plantings.	Euonymus range from ground-hugging cultivars to 40 feet in height, if the gardener chooses to encourage them on a structure. Full sun to heavy shade. Avoid wet soil. Can have problems with scale. Depending on the cultivar, yews grow from 3 feet to 20 feet high.
Yews (*Taxus*)	These are fine all-round plants, with a wide choice of varieties —all good. Easily pruned, provides year-round colour and doesn't lose attractive appearance as it gets older.	For sun or shade. Resistant to insects and disease. Needs good drainage.

We think that we shall never see a problem bigger than a tree

Some trees create unusual difficulties. These include birches, which are out of their element in our climate, and silver maples, which drop massive quantities of keys and produce a forest of seedlings that grow like weeds (they also suffer broken branches during summer storms and winter blizzards). We also have a problem with many varieties of crab-apple trees, which look wonderful for two weeks of the year, drop messy fruit for a month, and are susceptible to countless diseases and pests all year round.

But a garden isn't a garden without trees. We suggest you choose them with care—and select their location with even more care. Too many people underestimate the mature height of trees, and the cute little oak tree set near the living room window will eventually tower over the house and darken the windows. One rule of thumb, if you have the space to apply it: Plant any tree as far from your home as its maximum expected height.

For lots of enjoyment and little attention, it's hard to beat the trees we've selected for our first list. You might also consider our Honourable Mentions, if nothing on our First Team appeals to you.

Dave & Cathy's All-Time Favourite Low-Care Deciduous Tree List

Name	Description	Qualities
Downy serviceberry (*Amelanchier arborea*)	This medium-sized tree is a multi-season delight, with flowers in spring, thick foliage in summer, red leaves in fall and berries to attract birds. (The berries are supposed to be edible, but the birds consume them so quickly we've never had a chance to find out!)	15 to 25 feet high. Watch for mildew, scale and some insects.
European beech (*Fagus sylvatica* 'Purpurea Tricolour')	Believe it—there is no finer specimen tree. The one in our garden is overwhelming at first sight. Its purple leaves have a pinkish-rose border. Even the textured-grey bark is attractive, making this our clear favourite of all trees.	30 to 40 feet high. Few problems with pests or diseases, but it dislikes extreme heat. Slow grower.

Name	Description	Qualities
Japanese tree lilac (*Syringa reticulata* 'Ivory Silk')	A generally trouble-free lilac that serves as a specimen tree or street tree. Instead of a traditional lilac shape, this has a lovely rounded silhouette—a tree that's becoming very popular in our area.	20 to 30 feet high. Watch for scale and insects.
Katsura tree (*Cercidiphyllum japonicum*)	Leaves emerge in beautiful reddish-purple colour, changing to bluish-green in summer and on to yellow-apricot in fall. It deserves to be more popular in the southern areas of Canada.	40 to 60 feet high. Medium-to-fast grower. No pests or serious diseases.
Kousa dogwood (*Cornus kousa*)	A horizontal-branching tree with year-round appeal-white flowers in June, fruit and red leaves in the fall and attractive bark through the winter.	20 to 30 feet high. No serious pests. Tolerates shade.
Maidenhair tree (*Ginkgo biloba*)	A beautiful, fascinating tree (it hasn't changed in 150 million years) with fan-shaped leaves that turn yellow in fall. Very hardy, disease-resistant, slow-growing, attractive—but *big!* So take care where you place it. Dave grew ours from seed, which has created a deep relationship between it and him.	50 to 80 feet high. No serious pests.
Pagoda dogwood (*Cornus alternifolia*)	Interesting low-spreading tree with soft-green leaves in spring, turning reddish-purple in fall. The tiered horizontal branching habit gives a wonderful effect.	15 to 25 feet high. Watch for scale and insects.

The Honourable Mentions

AMUR MAPLE (*Acer ginnala*)

This compact maple—it rarely grows higher than 25 feet—makes a very nice specimen tree and even does well in containers, patios and courtyards. The handsome deep green leaves turn red and yellow in the fall, but trees in sunnier locations produce the most vivid colours. Fairly free of pest and disease problems.

JAPANESE MAPLE (*Acer palmatum* 'Bloodgood')

These delicate trees add an aristocratic touch to gardens and are ideal as accents or specimens. The Bloodgood type keeps its red-leaf colour

The tree that's virtually a living fossil

The ginkgo—sometimes called a "maidenhair tree"—is unique in its character, and has a fascinating history.

Native to China, the tree is basically extinct in the wild. Try as you might, you'll not find a forest of ginkgoes anywhere. Westerners visiting China in the seventeenth century discovered the trees growing in temple gardens and brought the seeds back to Europe. In Chinese the name for the tree translates as "tree with leaves like duck's foot," an apt description of the unusually shaped leaves. The Chinese also prized the seed growing within evil-smelling fruits produced by female ginkgoes, considering it a special delicacy. Archaeologists have discovered evidence of ginkgo trees, identical to those growing today, in fossils estimated to be over 100 million years old.

If you purchase a ginkgo from a nursery, ensure that you're getting a male specimen. I grew ours from a seed given to me by Cathy's aunt about thirty years ago. We don't know if it's a male or female (females don't start producing fruit for a few decades) —but we're keeping our fingers crossed.

—Dave

for an extended time. They can grow to 25 feet in height, but some varieties are much smaller. Protect from wind and direct sun, and water well in the first year. Not especially hardy.

LITTLELEAF LINDEN (*Tilia cordata*)

A very attractive shade tree, especially in cities and high-pollution areas, the linden deserves wider planting and should be among the first choices for those seeking a tall, elegant and attractive tree. Its dark shiny green leaves turn rich yellow in the fall, and it grows as high as 60 or 70 feet.

RED MAPLE (*Acer rubrum*)

A favourite showy tree whose leaves emerge with a reddish tinge before turning to dark green. The fall colour can range from yellow to a brilliant red. It is a fast grower—up to 12 feet high within 7 years—and can reach 60 feet in height, so locate it well away from your house. The tree's major enemies are leaf hoppers.

SAUCER MAGNOLIA (*Magnolia x soulangiana*)

In our opinion, this and the star magnolia (below) are the best of the magnolias. Both are more resistant to pests and diseases than others. For two to three weeks in spring, it will be the focus of beauty in your garden. Not overly large, it will reach 10 to 15 feet in 10 years. It's subject to a lot of pests and diseases, especially mildew and scale, but severe problems are uncommon.

STAR MAGNOLIA (*Magnolia stellata*)

This extremely showy tree looks especially nice against a red brick wall. The white star-shaped flowers are beautiful but delicate, and can be damaged in strong winds. It's a slow grower, rarely reaching more than 15 to 20 feet high, but fairly hardy—more resistant to pests and diseases, in fact, than the saucer magnolia (above).

The Secret Lives of Plants #5: The Horse Chestnut

Native Americans valued this tree for its medicinal properties. They used potions made from the nuts and bark to treat varicose veins and hemorrhoids, and crushed the nuts to make snuff for treating colds and rheumatism. Even today, some anti-inflammatory drugs are derived from the tree.

When we were young, children gathered the nuts, drilled holes through them, tied them on the end of shoelaces and challenged each other in a game. One child would dangle a chestnut-on-a-shoelace while the other would strike it by swinging another at it. They took turns doing this until the loser's chestnut shattered. Such were the days before video games . . .

Incidentally, it's called a horse chestnut because the nuts were used to treat respiratory ailments in horses.

Pruning trees: Don't try this at home

Trees small enough to reach with a sturdy stepladder are worth pruning yourself. Selective pruning promotes the tree's health and—very important—reduces maintenance from you in the long run.

Start by removing any dead or weak branches, as well as suckers growing from the base. Look for branches which cross in an "X" formation and are rubbing together, and remove all but one of them. (Remember to prune outside the branch collar—see page 108 for details.)

Avoid "topping" or round-over heading, which involves cutting the tree back equally on top and sides—it's like putting a bowl over your head and cutting off everything that doesn't fit inside it. Instead, thin out the tree to admit light inside its structure while retaining the tree's natural shape.

You can prune your own mature trees, if you wish. You can also take out your own appendix, we've been told. But we wouldn't advise doing either one. Leave any tree that cannot be comfortably pruned from the safety of a sturdy stepladder to experts. And ensure that your professional arborist will thin out the tree and not simply "top" it.

It can be expensive to have an arborist trim your tree, but it's worth it. Judge a tree-trimming service according to these qualities:

> • It is fully licensed, with bonding and insurance.
> • It has a professional affiliation, such as the National Arborist Association, the International Society of Horticulture and the Ontario Shade Tree Council.
> • It does not top mature trees. (Ask "Should I top my tree?" If they say "Yes," keep looking.)
> • It does not use spurs. People who climb telephone poles wear spurs on the sides of their boots. That's all right—telephone poles sprout very few leaves. But spurs can seriously damage a living tree. Good arborists use ropes and ladders.

Bright lights, dull squirrels

A professional acquaintance of ours decided to add a few new attractions to his garden—specifically to a large shade tree dominating his property.

He began by stringing lengths of miniature white lights among his branches. The effect, on summer evenings, was magical. So he bought and strung more. And more. By autumn he had purchased and strung every set of miniature white lights available from his local supplier. Thousands of white, twinkling stars played among the branches of his tree.

As spring approached, he anticipated throwing a switch and once again adding a fairyland atmosphere to his garden. On the first warm evening, he did just that. And nothing happened.

Close inspection revealed the problem: resident squirrels in the tree, either bored or hungry, had spent much of the winter chewing his light strings into useless bits, each about the length of a spaghetti strand.

—Dave & Cathy

CHAPTER 8

A PERENNIAL LIST
OF CHARACTERS . . .
AND VICE VERSA

To our great-grandparents, virtually all flowers were perennial. The idea of doling out hard-earned cash for annuals that last perhaps four months and demanded valuable time to feed, water and deadhead the plants would probably seem the height of folly.

Over the past couple of generations, however, annuals dominated perennials in many gardens. People had more spending money and more available time to fill the spaces around their new suburban houses with pansies, petunias, marigolds, snapdragons and the universal impatiens.

But for many reasons, gardeners have been rediscovering the appeal of perennials. Their choice has been enhanced by wonderful new cultivars, and many garden centres are responding with expanded display and sales areas dedicated to perennials.

Needless to say, we favour perennials for many reasons, especially their ability to provide us with beauty and pleasure year after year while making minimum demands on our time and energy.

This has led to a few problems for gardeners who are seeking a long-term meaningful relationship with perennials, instead of a shallow one-season-stand with annuals. The biggest problem is often simply deciding among the thousands of perennials available for most regions in Canada.

It's critical with perennials. When choosing annuals, your first consideration is probably limited to colour and size. The plants won't survive a first frost, so who needs to know their soil requirements, pruning needs, wintering habits and other traits? Knowing these qualities in perennials, and choosing plants according to the demands they may place on your time, is vital.

We could provide a boring chart with certain demands. But we thought a different approach would be more fun . . . and even more helpful.

Characters—loveable, tolerable and avoidable

Some people act anthropomorphic, which means they give human qualities to things that are clearly not human. Most people who practice anthropomorphism are owners of small dogs or precocious birds.

Well, we're anthropomorphic when it comes to some plants. We've become so familiar with many of them that they assume human-like personalities in our mind. Assigning these kinds of personalities to plants (they're all perennials, by the way) makes it easier to understand their nature and determine whether we want them as long-term inhabitants of our garden.

We offer their personality descriptions here in the same spirit. If a Prima Donna or two in your garden adds the same kind of spark your eccentric Uncle Alf adds to your dinner parties, be our guest. Mind you, this hasn't been easy. Selecting one type of plant over another for us is like asking Dave to choose his favourite kind of pie, or Cathy to name her favourite flavour of ice cream. But here we go anyway:

TRUSTED OLD FRIENDS

These are plants that get along with everyone, and whose presence we would miss if we didn't include them in our garden. They're all easy-care plants, and it's fun to arrange them in a group with one species taking over the blooming duties as another ceases blooming, all through the season.

Black-eyed Susan (*Rudbeckia fulgida*)—A descendant from native wildflowers, and a great colourful show-off in late summer. Give it a sunny location, rich moist soil, and it will do the rest.

Blue sage (*Salvia x superba*)—Blooms all summer long, with long deep-purple spikes of flowers growing out of scented grey-green foliage. Looks great with pink shrub roses or contrasting with yellow blooms.

Coral bells (*Heuchera micrantha 'Palace Purple'*)—These plants make ideal borders in sun or partial shade. We prefer the purple-leafed varieties for colour and contrast all season long. Many beautiful and unusual varieties are becoming available—including "Chocolate Ruffles." Small white flowers appear in early summer.

✓ **Cranesbill (*Geranium*)**—Not to be confused with what are called annual geraniums (actually *pelargonium*—another example where Latin botanical names can reduce confusion), these plants are available in dozens of varieties. Choose short, medium or tall with red, white, purple and pink blooms that provide a long blooming period in spring and early summer. Some of our favourites are *G. macrorrhizum* and *G. x cantabrigiense* 'Biokovo'; both are terrific ground covers and edging plants. Larger varieties to consider include *G. pratense* and *G. sanguineum*.

Day lilies (*Hemerocallis*)—Yes, they're the same plants that grow wild by the roadside, but many varieties are stunning in their colour and are reliable visitors year after year. 'Stella de Oro' is a dwarf variety with fragrant golden-yellow flowers and a darker-coloured throat in mid-summer. Day lilies will tolerate some shade, but you'll obtain more blooms in full sun.

Back **Elephant ears (*Bergenia cordifolia*)**—This is a great plant (long lived, few pests) with massive foliage (large rhubarb-sized leaves that turn red in the fall). In spring, tall thin stems rise from the plant to burst into delicate flowers ranging from pale pink to deep red. It makes a fine ground cover, or use it as a rock garden border. Locate it out of the hot afternoon sun and never cut it back—it's an evergreen perennial.

Lady's Mantle (*Alchemilla mollis*)—We love this tough little plant (it rarely grows higher than 10 inches) in sun or shade. In the rain, water droplets seem to sparkle on its scalloped green leaves, which are covered in a soft downy texture. Its tiny flowers are an unusual chartreuse colour. Great for edging.

 Liatris (*Liatris spicata*)—The tall, spiky blooms, in white or purple, last a very long time when cut for floral arrangements. For sunny locations.

Peony (*Paeonia*)—An old favourite with spectacular fragrant blossoms in early summer. Generally easy to get along with, but they go into a snit if moved or divided (rarely necessary) and may need hoops to hold the massive blooms upright.

Purple coneflower (*Echinacea purpurea*)—Bred from native wild-flowers, these are about as reliable as any flowering plant in your garden. The large blooms, with brown centre and drooping petals, last for several weeks in summer.

Showy stonecrop (*Sedum spectabile* 'Autumn Joy')—Long-lived, trouble-free and rated among the top ten perennials by some gardening books. It has a lovely shape all year round and blooms in early fall.

Silver sage (*Artemesia ludoviciana*)—Wonderful silver-grey foliage makes these excellent accent plants. Many varieties are available in various heights and textures. They love hot, well-drained sunny areas.

Tickseed (*Coreopsis verticillata* 'Moonbeam')—Use as an edging plant in full sun. From mid- to late summer, it shows off with delicate, pale yellow flowers, and is a favourite perennial for those familiar with it.

GENTLE GIANTS

Tall, almost oversized plants draw the eye up and provide an important shape to your garden. They have a place among low-lying rockery plants, blooming mid-sized flowers and shrubs. They're also fine to set at the back of a perennial bed or as specimen plants. Just be sure to give them room to spread out, and place some smaller plants or ground cover at their feet.

Goatsbeard (*Aruncus dioicus*)—These remind us of astilbes on hor-mones. They reach up to 6 feet high, with lacy leaves and, in mid-summer, creamy plumed flowers as big as your head. Plant them in partial shade at the back of your garden and keep the soil moist.

Joe Pye weed (*Eupatorium maculatum*)—Fans of this plant resent the term "weed"—and quite rightly too. Reaching to 6 feet in height, the plant displays wonderful large reddish-purple flowers from late sum-mer to frost. A bonus: the blooms have a rich vanilla scent. Plant in full sun. Incidentally, Joe Pye was a Native medicine man who believed the plant had magical healing powers.

Ligularia (*Ligularia dentata*)—We have come to love these somewhat strange, dramatic plants with their massive rhubarb-sized leaves. They prefer a cool, moist location in partial shade. Some gardeners suggest not planting them under large trees, which may give them too much competition for water. Look for *L. dentata* 'Desdemona'—purplish leaves with blooms resembling bright orange daisies; and *L. stenocephala* 'The Rocket'—deeply toothed leaves and flowers in spikes that resemble bottle brushes.

Meadowsweet (*Filipendula rubra* 'Venusta')—This is the plant for a boggy corner of your garden, although any rich moist soil will do. From early to mid-summer they'll display showy, deep-pink, fluffy flower heads with a lovely sweet scent. They are said to be Queen Elizabeth's favourite flower and, hey, if they're good enough for her . . .

Featherleaf rodgersia (*Rodgersia pinnata* 'Elegans')—Another moisture-loving plant that deserves wider recognition. After its creamy-white flowers have died away, it shows attractive bright-red seed heads that make interesting additions to floral arrangements.

Dealing with The Great Divide

Most perennials will eventually need dividing to keep them healthy and in full bloom. You'll know it's time to divide:
- *When the plants are obviously overcrowded.*
- *When plants in one clump generate noticeably fewer flowers.*
- *When the clump begins to die off in the middle.*

Dividing your perennials, when they need it, not only rejuvenates the plants but is also a form of propagation.

Plants can be divided in the fall, but we prefer doing it in the spring when new growth is visible. Spring also means warming soil, rain and mild temperatures—all encouraging growth and rejuvenation for the plant. In fall, the plants may not have enough time to establish roots before freeze-up.
- *Choose a day with dull, cloudy weather just before a rain, if possible, and ensure the soil is moist but not muddy.*
- *Loosen the soil, dig up the plant and make sure the root structure remains within the ball of soil.*
- *Shake off enough soil to look for natural places to make cuts or divisions.*
- *Check the roots and try to match them to a section of stalks growing out of the crown.*

> • *Try separating fibrous roots and rhizomes by pulling them apart with your hands, but don't be afraid to use a sharp knife on stubborn specimens.*
> • *Use a garden fork or shovel on large fibrous and fleshy roots on big, older plants if necessary.*
> • *Replant, making sure the hole is large enough to accommodate the roots without bending or trimming them. Add existing soil to equal parts compost or manure and peat moss. Set this mixture firmly around the roots and water thoroughly with a water-soluble transplant fertilizer (10-52-10). Keep watering through the growing season.*

Some perennials rarely, if ever, need dividing. They include:

Anemone

Astilbe

Blazing star (*Liatris*)

Bleeding heart (*Dicentra*)

Bugbane (*Cimicifuga*)

Bugleweed (*Ajuga*)

Columbine (*Aquilegia*)

Cranesbill (*Geranium*)

Day lily (*Hemerocallis*)

Meadowsweet-Filipendula

Hosta

Jacob's ladder (*Polemonium*)

Japanese spurge (*Pachysandra*)

Lady's mantle (*Alchemilla*)

Lily-of-the-valley (*Convallaria*)

Lupin (*Lupinus*)

Maltese cross (*Lychnis chalcedonica*)

Pinks (*Dianthus*)

Red-hot poker (*Kniphofid*)

Rose mallow (*Hibiscus*)

Snow-in-summer (*Cerastium*)

Try not to divide these plants—they dislike it:

Baby's breath (*Gypsophila*)

Blanket flower (*Gaillardia*)

Christmas rose (*Helleborus*)

Delphinium

Gas plant (*Dictamnus*)

Goatsbeard (*Aruncus*)

Monkshood (*Aconitum*)

Oriental poppy (*Papaver orientale*)

Peony (*Paeonia*)

Spurge (*Euphorbia*)

WELCOMED STRANGERS

Strangers to you, perhaps, but we've grown accustomed to the presence of these plants over the years. You may have to spend a little more time locating them and a little more care selecting and choosing the site, but we think they're worth it.

Christmas rose (*Helleborus niger* or *orientalis*)—The *orientalis* is sometimes called Lenten rose. While other people are admiring their crocuses and daffodils in early spring, we're raving about our *Helleborus* plants. Shade lovers, they prefer well-drained loamy soil. The Christmas rose often begins blooming under the snow, with large, cup-shaped, white flowers and leathery foliage that looks a little like a peony. The Lenten rose appears later and is probably easier to grow. These may take a little searching to locate, but they're well worth it.

Japanese anemone (*Anemone* x *hybrida*)—Plant these at the foot of your shrubs or behind some low-growing ferns. They explode in pink poppy-shaped blooms in late summer and fall, spreading to form a solid bed. Choose moist soil in a shady or partly sunny location and mulch well over its first winter. After that, they almost take care of themselves.

Japanese painted fern (*Athyrium niponicum* 'Pictum')—These do best in shade, but we've seen them survive in sunny locations, although the foliage fades somewhat. Typical fern-like leaves are olive green in colour with an interesting metallic grey and red texture.

Pincushion flower (*Scabiosa columbaria* 'Butterfly Blue' or 'Pink Mist')—These new varieties of old-fashioned flowers bloom from late spring to early fall. Both are dwarf varieties, ideal for borders. Deadhead for regular blooms. They need full sun and just average soil conditions. Try mixing the pink and blue varieties for dramatic effect.

Meadow rue (*Thalictrum delavayi* 'Hewitt's Double')—Although these can grow so tall they might require staking, their clouds of mauve flowers and lacy green foliage in late spring make them worth the effort. And don't banish them to the rear because of their height; they're a "see-through" plant, revealing other plants behind them. Originating in woodlands, they like rich, moist soil and sun or partial shade.

Variegated Jacob's Ladder (*Polemonium* 'Brise d'Anjou')—The fern-like green leaves are edged in gold, and when the blue flowers arrive in June, they're practically a surprise bonus. The foliage really is outstanding, and the plant should be given a prominent position as a focal point in a sunny or partly shady location.

Yellow archangel (*Lamiastrum galeobdolon* 'Herman's Pride')—This shade lover sits nicely among hostas, with its silver-veined pointed leaves. In mild regions, it remains an evergreen through winter.

Small yellow flowers make the plant an eye-catcher when in bloom. Note: Insist on the 'Herman's Pride' variety; others are inferior, in our opinion.

KISSING COUSINS

Plants don't have to be wildly exotic or difficult to locate in order to be different. Sometimes it's a matter of growing a special cultivar of a more familiar plant, to add interest and uniqueness to your garden. All of these, remember, are perennials.

False sunflower (*Heliopsis helianthoides*)—For rich yellow colour all through summer, this plant grows in poor soil, is drought-resistant, has virtually no pests and diseases, and makes great cut flowers. Hey, how much more can you ask for?

Ornamental onion (*Allium giganteum*)—Directly related to the ones you slice and chop, these produce truly spectacular purple flowers the size and shape of grapefruit, in June and July. Plant in odd groups—three, five, seven—in full sun.

Russian sage (*Perovskia atriplicifolia*)—The name fools you—it's not directly related to the herb sage but to the mint family. Nevertheless, it glows with lovely purple flowers in late summer, loves a hot and dry location in almost any kind of soil, and has a sweet, spicy fragrance.

Spurge (*Euphorbia*)—Directly related to the Christmas poinsettia, these are sun-loving, drought-tolerant plants. Look for donkey-tail spurge (*E. myrsinites*), as a rockery or wall plant, and cushion spurge (*E. polychroma*), which is much hardier in cold regions and produces bright white-yellow flowers in late spring.

Variegated obedient plant (*Physostegia virginiana* 'Variegata')— Choose this over the plain variety of obedient plant, which is un-interesting (and can become seriously invasive) compared with the variegated version. Red and white flowers, resembling miniature snapdragons, grow in four rows up a vertical flower stalk from mid-summer to fall. They grow to 36 inches high, so locate them in the middle or rear of your garden, in sun or partial shade. You may have to divide them every two or three years. Foliage is attractive all season long.

White bleeding heart (*Dicentra spectabilis* 'Alba')—If all bleeding hearts were white, they wouldn't be called bleeding hearts. This *Dicentra* is slightly less vigorous than its more familiar pink cousin. Choose a location with moist soil, total or partial shade, and away from the hot afternoon sun. *Dicentra formosa* has red or pink blossoms and beautiful fern-like foliage that remains attractive from spring to freeze-up. It's not as prolific as *spectabilis*, but it blooms all season long.

PRIMA DONNAS

Just as the name suggests, these plants may be a little demanding, a little rebellious and a little difficult getting to know them. But we forgive many of their bad manners in exchange for the beauty they bring to our garden.

Bearded iris (*Iris germanica*)—Who doesn't love irises? Their spectacular colours and interesting flower shapes appeal to everyone. But their beauty doesn't last long—barely a week—and many are susceptible to a borer that consumes the inner portion of the plant's rhizome. And they need dividing every three or four years, in August.

Canterbury bells/cup-and-saucer (*Campanula medium*)—The double-flowered form of canterbury bells displays blooms that look like cups on saucers—thus the name. (Kids love them.) The blue, white or pink flowers appear in early summer. They grow 24 to 36 inches high, are biennials and may need staking. In fact, the brittle stems may snap and break off if the plants are not staked.

Delphinium (*Delphinium elatum*)—The sight of our delphiniums in bloom never fails to generate "Oooohs!" and "Aaaahs!" from visitors. Their dramatic flower spikes at the back of one of our beds make a stunning sight in May and June. But be warned: They require rich, well-drained soil and need bone-meal feedings or additional compost material each spring. They also need feeding after their first blooming period to prompt a second wave of blooms later in the year. Unless well protected from wind, delphiniums always need their tops to be securely staked over the full height of the plant. Don't stop below the flower heads or the wind may snap them off. They're also subject to attack from cyclamen mites. Hey, it's not easy being beautiful. Plant them in a sunny spot that doesn't get too hot during the afternoon, and separate them well for good air circulation.

Foxglove (*Digitalis purpurea*)—Wonderful flowering plants that make everyone think of an English country garden, they're yet another vertical eye-catcher that will probably need staking. They're also biennials—not perennials—and while they may set seed themselves, they're not totally reliable so you may have to invest in new plants. The small, light seeds ride the wind easily, so you could find foxgloves popping up anywhere and everywhere in your garden. Choose locations with moist soil, in sun or open shade. Hints and Curious Facts Department: After the first blooming, cut the stalks before seeds form and you may get a second (but less significant) blooming in mid-summer.

Gasplant (*Dictamnus albus*)—Heavily scented, the blooms give off an inflammable oil. On a hot, still, muggy evening, place a lit match beneath a blossom and watch (or listen—you may only hear a soft puff). They take a year or two to settle in, and hate being moved. Their pink and white blooms, appearing in early summer, don't last very long either. But a healthy plant may live twenty years.

Lupin (*Lupinus* x *hybrida*)—Another breathtaking plant when in full bloom. They dislike acid soil (add some lime if you're not sure about the acidity) and don't like to have their feet wet, so choose a well-drained location. Lupins are very susceptible to attacks from aphids and other bugs, and the foliage looks scruffy after the plants finish blooming. Also, lupins don't last very long—about three or four years is average. Looking on the bright side, they are drought-tolerant.

Phlox (*Phlox paniculata*)—Very popular and very pretty during their mid-summer blooming season, but wow! Are they vulnerable to mildew! Don't overcrowd the plants. Good air circulation, plus light spraying with lime sulphur, will reduce the mildew problem. The plants also need to be divided regularly.

Rose mallow (*Hibiscus*)—Closer to shrubs than regular perennials, hibiscus need lots of summer heat to encourage their large red, rose, pink or white flowers to appear. They're also very late in emerging, and sometimes the first green shoots don't appear until late May with no blooms until August. Blooms last just one day, so for a good showing you need a large clump of plants. They may also require tying or staking.

These favourites of ours do well in shady areas. They may not be as dramatic as roses and other sun-loving plants, but they bring their own charm, and most require little attention once they're well established.

Astilbe (*Astilbe*)—Everyone loves these plants for their delicate foliage and their plumes of flower heads in white and pastel shades of red, orange, lavender and pink. With more than a hundred varieties available, try mixing several in a mass planting for a range of colours and blooming times. (Our favourite is *simplicifolia* 'Sprite'—it's compact in size, has especially dainty foliage, blooms later than others and is even more pest-resistant.) Choose an area in partial shade, preferably near some evergreens (they prefer acidic soil). Astilbes have quite an appetite for nutrients, so you may want to add top dressings of compost from time to time.

Hostas should be your first choice for shady areas. Mix several varieties for maximum beauty, but avoid variegated types if slugs are a serious problem.

Side

Hosta (*Hosta*)—If you have shade, you must have hostas. That's our rule, and we're sticking with it. Hardy hostas, by the way, are more tolerant of sun (preferably the morning rays) than many people believe, so you don't need to restrict them to the deepest, darkest corners of your

Must hosta always be a salad for slugs?

Hostas aren't just popular with people—they're totally adored by slugs, whose appetite for their leaves is the plant's biggest drawback. The white areas of variegated hostas seem to be real delicacies to slugs and snails.

What to do?

The slimy creatures don't like the thick, fleshy leaves of some hostas and may leave them alone altogether. There's always the beer-in-a-saucer trick (the slugs crawl in and drown or become too drunk to crawl back out, we're not sure.)

Other tactics: upturned half-grapefruit rinds (the sugar attracts the creatures, the acid kills them); ashes, sand, eggshells or sandpaper spread around the plants; or copper strips available from some garden supply dealers placed around beds to deter them.

If you have a slightly sadistic bent, venture out in the evening, when the slugs come out to feed, with a flashlight and a salt shaker. A dash of salt on their exposed bodies quickly dissolves them into something we don't want to think about.

—Dave & Cathy

garden. Mix several varieties in a bed as ground cover or to frame taller, showier plants such as astilbes. Hosta even looks attractive planted in straight rows, so consider using it to edge a path or walkway. We especially like 'Halcyon' with deep blue-green leaves, 'August Moon', a gold-leaf varietal; and 'Frances Williams', whose huge textured green leaves have wide yellow margins.

Lungwort (*Pulmonaria longifolia*)—They need virtually no maintenance, love shade and have interesting spotted foliage. In spring, small white or blue flowers appear. Use as a plant-and-forget ground cover, set among hostas and spring bulbs.

Monkshood (*Aconitum napellus*)—A showy plant for the back of a border in a cool, moist area. Showy spikes of flowers in blue, violet or pink appear during summer or fall. Warning: Wash you hands after handling the roots of this plant; they are very poisonous.

Primrose (*Primula*)—Usually considered an English flower unsuited to our cold winters, several varieties of primrose do very well here, providing plenty of spring colour in a wide variety of colours lasting for several weeks. They prefer shady or partly shaded cool locations, with rich moist soil (plant them in front of evergreen shrubs and add lots of peat moss and compost). On the prairies and in northern regions, apply an extra-thick layer of mulch to help them through winter.

Solomon's seal (*Polygonatum multiflorum*)—A wonderfully trouble-free plant that does well in either dry or moist shade. In spring, creamy-white flowers hang from graceful stems and rich textured green leaves. Undemanding and slow-growing, it looks best among hostas and beneath evergreen trees.

Turtlehead (*Chelone obliqua*)—These showy plants add colour to late-summer gardens. They do well in shade or partial shade, and tolerate heavy clay soils. The strong plants grow 16 to 24 inches tall, with dark pink or purple flowers on spiky stems. The flower are shaped like (surprise!) turtle heads.

Starting a perennial bed

A common mistake many beginning gardeners make is simply being too ambitious. Perennial flower beds are so attractive, in so many ways, that you may find yourself encountering problems—for example, growing confused over the needs (and identity!) of many plants in your garden.

We suggest you start with a reasonably sized flower bed—perhaps 100 to 120 square feet in total area. A perennial bed that's too small won't permit you to obtain the spacing that makes perennials so interesting (please don't plant them in rows!), and a larger bed may be too much to handle the first year.

Choose plants from our list of Trusted Old Friends (page 121) for sunny areas, and Shady Ladies (page 130) for spots receiving little or no sun. (As an alternative to starting a perennial bed from scratch, set the perennials among some existing low shrubs or small evergreens.) A word to the wise: Check the estimated size of each plant at maturity, and leave sufficient room for it to grow over the years. Until the plants are full-sized, fill in spaces between them with annuals and mulch.

Much of the fun and creativity of perennial gardening comes from mixing various sizes, shapes, colours, textures and bloom times to obtain a bed in which "something always seems to be happening." This is not going to occur in the first year, or perhaps even for the first two or three years. Don't despair—among all its appealing qualities, gardening promotes a long-term outlook. As you become more acquainted with the plants and the location, you'll constantly find ways to improve the garden year by year. Keep a record of the plants you love, the ones you merely tolerate and the varieties you want to add in the future.

It's worth reviewing a few basic guidelines at this point:

- Perennials can be planted in either spring or early fall. We prefer spring, because it gives the plant an entire season to become established. If you choose fall, be sure to allow enough time for the plant to start setting roots before winter freeze-up.
- Try setting the plants in groups of three—it's visually more appealing.
- Give the plant a good start with a feeding of water-soluble transplant fertilizer (10-52-10). Later in the season, you could feed it with 15-30-15 or 20-20-20 fertilizer, but this won't be necessary if you have prepared the soil with lots of good compost.
- During the first season, water the plant frequently and deeply. Your goal is to encourage the roots to extend as far as possible below the plant, making it more resistant to drought problems.
- Avoid watering late in the day; water left on the foliage can encourage disease problems. Early morning is best.
- Soaker hoses save time and energy, and provide water to plants more effectively than overhead sprinklers do. Just be sure to lay the hoses in place during spring, before the plants grow too large.
- After plants have flowered, deadheading them often encourages more blooms later in the season.
- When foliage begins to look ugly, simply cut back yellow, black or brown shoots, leaves or stems to keep the garden looking attractive.
- During fall clean-up, make a decision on the plants to cut back. You have three alternatives:
  1. Cut back most perennials to about a foot in height. This enables the dead shoots to catch and trap snow, prevents them from looking raggedy in winter winds, and alerts you to their location next spring.
  2. Some perennials, such as sedum and Annabelle hydrangea manage to look attractive in the dead of winter, and are rarely damaged by winds, so we avoid cutting them at all.
  3. Flower seed heads from coneflowers, black-eyed Susans and others attract birds to the garden in winter, so we leave them standing as well.

• When the first bulbs are peeking out of the ground, it's time for spring clean-up. Cut back old growth, leave new growth intact, divide older perennials if necessary and put down a layer of compost, working it into the soil around plants.

• Once the perennials are established (except for some Prima Donnas, such as delphiniums), that's all the feeding they receive. After that, it's survival of the fittest.

Take them, please!

We knew a wonderful woman whose enthusiasm for gardening almost matched our own. Like all gardeners, she enjoyed sharing her bounty with others. One season, she had a magnificent show-ing of marigolds in a large bed of her garden. The following spring, the area was massed with tiny green seedlings—her beautiful marigolds had self-seeded!

They needed thinning out, of course. But tossing the extra plants on her compost heap would be such a waste. So she duti-fully collected small pots and carefully transplanted the seedlings from her garden into the pots. Then she distributed the plants to everyone in her neighbourhood, hoping they would enjoy this year's crop of marigolds as much as she had enjoyed them the previous summer.

Everyone thanked her profusely and chose special locations for their flower plants, self-seeded from her previous year's marigolds.

You may have guessed the truth.

The seedlings weren't marigolds, but a particularly nasty weed, and for weeks everyone was feeding, watering and coaxing these little rascals toward maturity—until reality and the truth arrived.

Every year since, everyone in the neighbourhood makes a point of buying all their bedding plants from the local nursery.

—Dave & Cathy

CHAPTER 9

ANNUALS, BULBS AND CONTAINERS

Our goal from the beginning has been to reduce the effort needed to create and maintain the garden of your dreams. But the garden of everyone's dreams includes at least a few ABCs—annuals, bulbs and containers—and, except for spring-flowering bulbs, these are basically not low-maintenance items.

The idea behind this chapter is to explore and suggest ways you can add these elements to your garden without adding hours of trouble and toil. Once again, it's mostly a matter of preparation and selection.

Annuals? Well, if you really insist ...

Earlier, we compared annuals with fast food like cheeseburgers and French fries—fun to have, but you wouldn't want a steady diet of them.

More important, you don't need the time and effort to provide the special care and attention many annuals demand, compared with most perennials. When you reflect on the way that annuals grow, it's easier to appreciate why they are susceptible to many problems.

Perennials are a little like laid-back people. They get new life in the spring, enjoy themselves in the summer, and when winter threatens they retreat from the cold and wait for spring to return.

Annuals, on the other hand, are manic depressives. They want to get going at a frantic pace with the first promise of spring, and soon they're bloomin' fools, carrying on with bees and butterflies, producing off-spring as though there is no tomorrow. Which is pretty close to the truth. Comes the first serious frost, and most annuals are good for nothing but the compost pile.

With that kind of lifestyle, it's no wonder that annuals tend to be more prone to certain problems, and more demanding of your time and attention. Still, some annuals possess traits that enable you to enjoy their prime benefits—instant, summer-long colour—without tolerating the disadvantages. These are plants that, for the most part, have good resistance against pests and disease, grow densely enough to smother weeds and require little deadheading or other fussing.

Ageratum (*Ageratum houstonianum*)—Also known as 'Floss Flower', these do well in sunny locations and ordinary garden soil. They make great edging plants, in lovely shades of blue.

Blue salvia (*Salvia farinacea*)—Another plant that seems to look its best among most other colours, these become more attractive as the season progresses. Set them in full sun.

Coleus (*Coleus blumei*)—Their colourful leaves are almost standard as edgings in shady corners of many gardens. We think they look better if you pinch off the flowers.

Cosmos (*Cosmos bipinnatus*)—They need deadheading from time to time, but the brightly coloured flowers, beautiful foliage and long blooming season make them worth the trouble for us. Full sun and ordinary garden soil do the trick.

Dusty miller (*Senecio cineraria*)—The silvery foliage sets off brightly coloured plants around them. Besides being very drought-resistant, they're also very tough and can sometimes survive a Canadian winter. Sun or partial shade.

Fibrous or Wax Leaf begonias (*Begonia semperflorens*)—Beautiful white pink or rose blooms that never need deadheading. Try the new Lotto Pink variety, with extra-large pink blooms. They do well in sun or shade.

Geraniums (*Pelargonium*)—The old faithful. More colour for sun and partial shade.

Gloriosa daisy (*Rudbeckia hirta* 'Indian Summer')—Why choose an annual rudbeckia when there are so many perennial varieties available? Because the blooms are huge—as large as 5 or 6 inches across—this is a real show-stopper.

Our prejudice against annuals can be shattered by show-stoppers such as Gloriosa Daisy (*Rudbeckia hirta* "Indian Summer").

Impatiens (*Impatiens walleriana*)—How else can you get easy colour in shady areas? But please don't overdo it. There are so many other, more interesting plants to choose from.

Plume Cocksomb (*Celosia argentea plumosa*)—For late-summer shades of fiery red, orange and even deep pink, in sunny locations. Our favourite cultivars are 'Pink Castle', 'New Look' and 'Apricot Brandy'.

Snapdragons (*Antirrhinum majus*)—Yet another old favourite that most everyone likes to see. In the spirit of Rusty Rake gardening, we recommend the shorter varieties that never need staking. For sunny locations.

Spider flower (*Cleome spinosa*)—An unusual late-blooming plant that grows to 3 or 4 feet or so in height, with strange-looking pink and white flowers on a slender, vertical stem. As the flowers are pollinated, the centre stamen extends 2 to 3 inches with seed pods on the tips. Plant in full sun and water regularly; they're good at self-seeding.

Vinca (*Catharanthus rosea*)—Compact, branching plants with periwinkle-like flowers in white or pale-to-deep pink colours. Not to be confused with Vinca major and Vinca minor, which are perennials, not

The gardener as exterior decorator

Have you ever walked into a healthy, well-maintained garden and felt . . . well, unimpressed or unmoved? It's as though something is missing, but you just can't put your finger on it. Other gardens, meanwhile, impress you beyond the size, spacing, health and appearance of the plants. They actually create an emotional response that makes you want to stay and wrap yourself up in the special mood you're feeling.

The difference, in many cases, is colour. Along with other qualities, the gardeners have selected and placed plants according to their colour impact.

This may not have much to do with keeping the rake rusty and unused at the back of the garden shed, but it can add an extra measure of enjoyment to your garden, leaving your friends even more impressed with your green thumb—even if they're not sure why.

Here are six ways to apply colour in your garden. If you're using easy-care annuals to create the mood, you can change it each year if you wish.

1. For a relaxing mood, keep it cool. Flowers and foliage in tones dominated by blue, purple, rose, pink and white are restful to the eye and soul.

2. For drama, get hot. Warm and hot colours—crimson, orange and yellow—stimulate the eye, creating a sense of excitement.

3. For balance, contrast hot and cool. This adds interest to cool colours and subtlety to the hotter tones. Yellow blooms will brighten a blue and purple flower bed, and blue adds calm to a riot of red and orange flowers.

4. Unify with whites. Locate groupings of white flowers among your beds of mixed or contrasting colours. The white blossoms will help the overall effect.

5. In dry, sunny areas plants with silver foliage—such as Artemesia—will help break up a sea of green leaves.

6. Much of the fun lies in changing the colour scheme of your garden with the changing seasons. This takes some planning, of course, but you can have a predominance of pinks and blues during spring, and enjoy shades of gold, copper and bronze in the fall.

annuals (plant names can be very confusing). A great edging plant that needs no deadheading. Likes sun or partial shade.

Wheat Celosia (*Celosia spicata*)—We especially recommend a new cultivar called 'Purple Flamingo', which can grow three feet high, so give it room. It likes rich, moist soil and sun.

Biennials—Non-conformists in the garden

Neither annual nor perennial, biennial plants extend their lives through two summers and a single winter. Sprouting the first year, they store enough food in their root system before becoming dormant in winter and returning in spring to blossom and set their seeds. Then they're gone for good—usually. Biennials sow new seeds to begin the cycle over again, but not always in the same place. So be prepared for surprises now and then. Many biennials, including foxglove (*Digitalis purpurea*), Sweet William (*Dianthus barbatus*) and forget-me-not (*Myosotis sylvatica*) self-sow so effectively that you probably think they're perennials. Other biennials worth adding to your garden include Canterbury bells (*Campanula medium*) and some hollyhocks (*Alcea rosea*).

A grab-bag of ideas for annuals

• *While waiting for your perennials to establish themselves, start a large bed of* Rudbeckia hirta *'Indian Summer'—massive blooms in vibrant colour to draw lots of raves from friends.*

• *Resist rows. With rare exceptions, plant all flowers—including annuals—in beds or clumps.*

• *Annuals in a perennial garden are like cushions in a living room. Spot them here and there for colour; consider them accessories, not furniture.*

• *The new 'Purple Wave' petunias make fabulous ground-cover plants, spreading profusely to fill in bare spots.*

Bulbs—Nature makes it almost too easy

For many people, spring plants from bulbs are the first experience they have with plants that are perennial in nature. Spring bulbs are virtually trouble-free. Dig a hole in the fall, drop in the bulb (try to place them root-side down) and relax until spring. As the snows withdraw, you'll be rewarded with perky little crocuses and snowdrops, followed by daffodils, narcissus, anemones, and of course, tulips. Best of all, they'll almost certainly return year after year, even if they're totally ignored when the great burst of later-blooming plants finally arrives.

With a little preparation, you can harvest much more enjoyment. The flowers of most spring-blooming plants are short-lived, so plant mixtures of early, mid-season and late-blooming varieties for a longer season of colourful flowers from your bulbs. And don't plant them in rows, like soldiers; all blooms from bulbs look better in groups or beds. Remember, as well, that the green foliage must remain after the blooms have died or been harvested. Cutting or removing the leaves too early— before they turn yellow and wither away—will prevent the plant from building sufficient food for next year's blooms.

Here are some other suggestions that you might not have considered when planting bulbs:

> • Choose your bulbs carefully, and try to select them yourself. Reject any bulbs that have soft spots or visible mould.
> • Don't plant them all alone in an open area. When the blooming period is completed, the yellowing foliage is unattractive. Set them among shrubs or perennials, which will mature and draw attention from the dying leaves (daffodils look especially attractive when set under trees).
> • Don't choose wet, poorly drained areas or the bulbs may rot.
> • Most bulbs prefer sun or open shade. If you avoid setting them in an exceptionally hot area—such as against a south-facing wall—the blooms will last several days longer.
> • In colder areas or in sandy soil, plant bulbs four to five times deeper than their height. In other soil and regions, you may plant them two to three times their height but generally deeper is better. Add some compost and bone meal to the soil and water well.

Bulbs you might never have thought of

Spring blooms aren't the only flowers that begin as bulbs. Lilies are fine summer flowers, adding plenty of dramatic colour and sweet aromas to your garden. Best of all, they are as reliable and maintenance-free as any perennial flowering plant in your garden.

By the way, we're referring here to (sorry about the Latin) genus *Lilium*. This is to distinguish them from other plants with "lily" in their name—day lily, water lily, calla lily, canna lily and even lily-of-the-valley.

We plant lilies in the fall, giving them time to set their roots before winter arrives. Choose a sunny, well-drained location; if water collects in the area, the bulbs will rot. We also crowd them a little, planting three to five bulbs per square foot. Mix several varieties and you're likely to have blooms from June through to September. Taller varieties with oversized blooms may need staking; deadhead the flowers after blooming but leave the foliage intact for the plant to build nourishment.

Lilies are highly resistant to disease and pests, require no special attention and multiply rapidly. This last quality means you may want to divide them every few years.

The most commonly available lilies are defined as Asiatics, trumpets and Orientals.

Asiatics are both the earliest and the most colourful of all lilies. The flowers—many with spots or "brush-strokes"—cover a wide range of colours, shapes and sizes.

Don't believe everything you read in books—except this one

The experts say Easter lilies (Lilium longiflorum) won't survive a Canadian winter, and we used to believe them. But one year, just to be contrary, we planted some Easter lilies in our garden. The plants had arrived as gifts and, after waiting for them to finish blooming, we set the bulbs and foliage in a suitable spot.

The following spring, green shoots emerged on schedule and the plants seemed as contented as any other in our garden. Maybe more so—we counted forty-three blooms on one plant!

This was several years ago, and the lilies still return each spring. On warm evenings, their scent fills the air in the garden.

Of course, if you trust most gardening books, they'll advise you to forget about growing Easter lilies in most of Canada. But trust us—we can do it, and perhaps you can too.

—Dave & Cathy

Trumpets can reach to 6 feet in height and look wonderful set in masses among shrubs. Their range of colours is not as broad as the Asiatics, but they make up for it with rich fragrance. They may require staking, however.

Orientals are late-bloomers, showing their large, fragrant star-shaped flowers in August or September. If you have rhododendrons, consider planting oriental lilies among them; they make good neighbours. Orientals are not quite as hardy as other lilies, and it's a good idea to mulch them heavily in winter.

High-maintenance bulbs and tubers

Canna lilies, dahlias, gladiola and tuberous begonias also begin as bulbs or tubers, and can also add a good deal of summer colour to your garden. But, especially compared with spring bulbs and lilies, these are hardly low-maintenance plants.

Their bulbs and tubers must be dug up after the first killing frost, dried, stored in peat moss in a cool location over the winter and re-planted in spring.

If these plants hold enough appeal to you, they may be worth the effort. Or, if you prefer, you can treat them like annuals and be satisfied with one season's worth of blooms from your investment. It's up to you.

Confession time: In spite of their demands, we have grown canna lilies in containers, using them as a dramatic and effective mid-summer patio screen. Their height—over six feet in the containers—their luxu-riant foliage and beautiful red blooms worked perfectly in our barbecue area, and when fall arrived it was easier to remove the bulbs from the containers than from deep in the ground.

Speaking of containers . . .

Like annuals and bulbs, containers are not low-maintenance garden items. Still, they can fill a role in almost any garden. We suggest you don't rely on them too much, and apply a few Rusty Rake techniques to reduce container maintenance to a minimum.

You'll want containers to bring plants and colour to difficult areas such as a large tiled courtyard or patio. They're also good as stop-gaps where you're just beginning to create a new garden and your bevy of perennials and shrubs aren't yet at their best.

To make use of them in this way, and still keep your gardening chores to a minimum, here are our suggestions:

- In containers, use an equal mixture of screened compost, peat moss and perlite or vermiculite (available from garden supply dealers) instead of soil from your garden. You can often purchase ready-mixed container soil, if you prefer. The mixture will hold moisture better than ordinary garden soil.
- Set a layer of gravel inside the container for drainage before adding the soil mixture.
- Don't fill the container completely; leave an inch or so of space beneath the rim to contain overflow when watering the plants.
- Use large containers to reduce the frequency of watering your container plants.
- Give the plants a boost with an initial feeding of transplant fertilizer —10-52-10.
- Instead of scattering container plants around your yard, reduce the time needed to water the plants by setting the containers in groups. They'll also look more attractive this way.
- Even with large containers, expect to water frequently—every two or three days in mid-summer, for containers set in direct sun—and be sure to check the soil for moisture regularly.
- Along with water, your container plants need regular feeding as well. We mentioned Dave's Rule earlier, and it applies especially to container plants: add small amounts of water-soluble plant food— 15-30-15 is best—to your watering can every time. We also use a granular, slow-release fertilizer that's especially made for container plants. It's available at most garden centres. One feeding should carry the plant about half-way through the growing season before water-soluble food is needed.
- While you're away on a summer vacation, your perennials will probably do fine, but your container plants will require regular attention. Enlist a friend, relative or neighbour to feed and water them.
- Never reuse the same container soil mixture the following year. For small containers—less than 1 foot in diameter—replace the soil mixture completely. Larger containers may need only the top half of the soil replaced each year.
- Containers work well with low-maintenance shade-loving plants like coleus, fibrous begonias, ivy, impatiens and dusty miller.
- We move many of our tropical house plants outdoors in summer, setting them in containers. They thrive in the natural warmth and humidity of summer. But give them time to acclimate—place them

outside on a mild day, out of the wind and direct sun. Over a two-week period, gradually move them into a location where they receive more sun each day. Most house plants thrive under half-sun/half-shade conditions.

• For hanging containers from pergolas, arbours and verandas, use baskets made of sphagnum moss or coconut fibre instead of plastic. They look more attractive—an important point since hanging containers are much more apparent than those on the ground. Remember, too, that hanging containers will likely require more frequent watering thanks to the drying effect of the wind.

The Secret Lives of Plants #7: Peony

Although it originated in Asia, the peony takes its name from the Greek god Apollo. In disguise, Apollo would pose as the physician Paeon and serve as physician to the other gods. The peony was said to have unusual curative powers for epilepsy and insanity, and mothers in medieval England often fastened peony roots around the necks of babies to help them teethe and avoid convulsions.

Container types—advantages and drawbacks

Stone and concrete containers are the most attractive—and expensive, we hasten to add. When filled with soil, they're virtually impossible to move, so locate them carefully before filling and planting. And remember that you'll have to empty the containers completely before winter sets in to avoid cracking. If the containers lack drainage holes, be sure to invert them over winter to prevent damage from ice formation.

Pottery and terracotta pots are just as attractive as stone—and just as susceptible to winter damage if left filled with soil.

Plastic containers are inexpensive and hold moisture better. They don't breathe like a good terracotta pot, but you needn't worry about removing soil before winter either. Lately, we've seen some plastic containers that closely resemble terracotta pots, including having classic sculpture and relief patterns on the side, making them much more attractive.

Wooden barrels add a nice rustic appearance to a garden, especially when spilling over with easy-care old-fashioned annuals such as nasturtiums. Like stone and terracotta pots, they're much too heavy to be moved easily when soil has been added.

Container plants—choosing the best

By choosing the plants for your containers with some care, you can reduce the amount of time needed for chores such as deadheading and constant watering. Here are a few of our favourites. They provide the colour, texture and rich foliage needed in containers:

- Surfinia petunias and new 'Wave' petunias almost overcome our prejudice against these normally high-maintenance annuals. The Wave variety hangs nicely over the edge instead of growing upright.
- New 'Prism Sunshine' petunias, with very bright creamy-yellow blooms, are also fine for containers. Best of all, they need very little deadheading.
- Licorice plants (*Helichrysum petiolatum*) add attractive silver-green foliage to bloomers.
- Add ivy to your containers—*Hedera helix* is a good choice—for interesting green foliage.
- Dahlberg daisies are a favourite of ours for container plantings.
- Bacopa, Abutilon or 'Flowering Maple', Scaevola or 'Fan-flower', lobelia, and of course geraniums (*Pelargonium*) all make fine container plants. Try mixing these in various combinations for different effects.

Try experimenting with various combinations until you come up with something that works for you. Finally, don't overlook herbs for container plantings. Set two or three containers of chives, basil, rosemary, parsley, thyme and others near your kitchen door and snip off whatever you need for recipes or as a garnish.

Christmas at the Cummins': Mother's stuffing turkey, Father's planting bulbs.

I had an aunt who worked at a large farm-and-garden supply dealer's. At the end of every autumn selling season, knowing our love of gardening, she would gather all the store's unsold spring bulbs—the ones rejected by shoppers—and package them for Dave.

One year, she made the bulbs his Christmas gift. As it happened, it was an especially mild Christmas season, so Dave set out for the garden with spade, bone meal and dozens of bulbs.

Our children were quite young then, and I seem to recall someone phoning to wish us all a Merry Christmas. My son answered the phone and during the conversation said: "We're playing with our toys, Mom's stuffing the turkey and Dad's out in the garden, planting bulbs for spring."

Anyone who knew us well—even back then—wouldn't have been overly surprised.

—Cathy

CHAPTER 10

THYME IS ON YOUR SIDE

It is impossible to discuss gardening without mentioning vegetables. Tending beautiful flowers and attractive shrubs returns a good deal of joy, but we admit there is something special about walking into your garden on a late summer morning, plucking a ripe tomato off a plant you've raised from a seedling, and biting into its fresh, juicy sweetness. If you have raised the plant according to strictly organic guidelines, it's even more satisfying to know you've managed to avoid any risks associated with pesticides, insecticides and some chemical additives.

But . . .

Like your lawn, vegetables can demand volumes of your time, attention and labour, especially if you want both good appearance and high yields. Many people consider gardening for beauty as frivolous; they'll keep a few flowers around for show, but to them gardening means a bountiful harvest in late summer and fall, facing winter with a root cellar full of squash and potatoes and a canning shelf crowded with preserves, all the product of their own garden.

Yet we have also seen sad-sack vegetable gardens begin with high hopes in May, and collapse among weeds and sick plants in August. What happened? Usually, it has been a matter of underestimating the time and attention it takes to maintain a good-sized vegetable garden. Controlling weeds, banishing insects, watering regularly, plus nurturing, pruning, thinning and staking—not to mention fighting off bandits such as raccoons, squirrels, possums and rabbits—can put quite a dent in your time and energy.

Just to make things more difficult, farmers have become so productive and their distribution systems so efficient that it makes very little sense to grow your veggies as a cost-saving measure. At the height of the season, when vegetable prices are low and selection is great, it's difficult to justify trekking out and spending a few hours in the hot sun labouring over your backyard plot.

We hasten to add that we raise vegetables ourselves. Always have, with varying success (read our adventures with raccoons—page 157—for a full confession). But our focus in this book is to reduce time and effort while increasing the pleasure from your garden, and with vegetables, that's always a challenge.

One suggestion: Many popular herbs and spices are not only attractive and easy to grow but are far tastier when fresh than are the dried versions you buy from supermarkets. Sage, thyme, basil, chives, rosemary, parsley and others can satisfy your need to grow something edible and fresh while avoiding the intense attention needed by vegetable crops.

Reviewing the basics:
Vegetables have special needs

High-yield vegetables such as tomatoes, beans and lettuce lead short, intense lives. Most plants can take their time building food in their roots and foliage on their stems, but veggies have just two or three months to achieve the same goal. Keep this in mind, and it puts a number of things in proper perspective leading, we hope, to producing more vegetables with less effort.

> • *Most vegetables need sun—lots of it.* Choose a location that receives at least six hours of direct sun daily—any less and your plants may be spindly and unproductive.
> • *Feed your vegetable plants well now and they'll feed you well later.* Some flowering plants can thrive in poor soil, but vegetables cannot. Each year before planting, spread a blanket of compost or well-rotted manure on your garden about 2 or 3 inches thick before turning the earth over. Mix the compost or manure to a depth of 6 or 8 inches before planting.
> • *Choose between rows and beds.* Planting your vegetables in rows (make each no wider than the spread of your arms for easy access) enables you to reach the plants and provides good air circulation between them. Beds will increase the number of plants you can grow, but tending them may be difficult and poor air circulation encourages rust, mildew and other problems.

• *Follow the sun.* If you plant in rows, lay them out running from east to west. This way, they'll receive maximum exposure to the sun's rays all day long.

• *Remember that vegetable plants love to drink but they hate wet feet.* You'll have to provide some form of irrigation for your vegetable plants —they'll need at least an inch of water a week—so try to locate your vegetable garden near a water source. Vegetables cannot tolerate standing water, which means you'll have to eliminate areas where water collects after a rain. A suggestion: Invest in a soaker hose, which dribbles water into the ground, and snake it among your plants. Connect it to a faucet, leave it in place all season long (conceal the hose leading to it with mulch or perennials) and during dry spells simply turn on the faucet for an hour or so. Faucet "splitters" are available at most garden supply centres. They enable you to feed and control two different watering systems from one faucet, so you can separate your vegetable garden watering needs from your perennial garden and lawn watering needs without installing a second faucet.

• *Some gardeners add a few flowers for aesthetic and practical reasons.* They dress up their veggie plot by spotting blooms here and there or on the perimeter, in the hope that the blooms will attract beneficial insects such as bees, ladybugs and lacewings. If you want to do this—we don't, by the way—you might choose nasturtiums, which also happen to be edible. (We set dill and chives among our vegetable plants from time to time because the herbs are claimed to be beneficial in many ways. So far, the jury is still out.)

• *Mulch for weed control, appearance and plant-feeding.* Many vegetable gardeners use a heavy mulch of straw between their plants. Along with suppressing weeds and retaining moisture, the straw mulch slowly breaks down to create an extra feeding of compost.

• *Schedule your harvests in advance.* Groups of fresh leaf lettuce and radishes should be planted two weeks apart. Both are good cool weather crops, so you can begin radishes about five weeks before the last frost of spring, and put lettuce in the ground as soon as the soil can be worked. By planning ahead you'll have a regular flow of vegetables instead of one overwhelming harvest.

• *Rotate your crops.* If you are cultivating large beds or rows, avoid planting the same vegetables in the same spot two years in succession. Some plants—members of the cabbage family, for example— should not be planted in the same soil for at least two or three years. By avoiding successive plantings you'll prevent damage from soil-borne insects and diseases remaining in the same location. These pests attack specific plants, so this year's lettuce microbes will be thwarted next year if you plant beans or carrots. Suggestion: Draw a plan of your vegetable garden plot and record the location of each vegetable so you can avoid planting it in the same soil next year.

• *Perennial vegetables are great.* If you like rhubarb or asparagus, consider introducing them into your garden. Asparagus prefers sandy soil and takes two to three years to become established, but you'll be harvesting crops for years with little care or concern. Stop harvesting when the plants grow spindly. They'll mature into large, feathery asparagus ferns which you can cut later and add to flower arrangements.

• *Broccoli in barrels?* Friends of ours grow vegetables in half-barrels, with flowers planted at their base. Lifting the plants off the ground may also protect them from attacks by snails, slugs and rabbits.

The Secret Lives of Plants #8: Nettles

The word "nettle" usually conjures up a vision of stinging nettle, a tough weed with fascinating qualities. (Dead nettle—Lamium maculatum—is an attractive ground cover that grows readily in poor soil and partial shade.)

Stinging nettle has been used for everything from a hair restorer to a styptic application to stop bleeding. In Scotland, it was prized over flax to make linens; Romans beat paralyzed limbs with the plant to restore life; and Britons made tea from it as an antidote to poison.

Native Americans brewed nettles to drink the liquid to cure chills and jaundice. A nettle leaf on the tongue was claimed to stop nosebleeds and applied to the bites of a mad dog as a cure for rabies.

In the garden, stinging nettle is claimed to promote the production of vegetables and the quality of herbs; some gardeners steep a pound of nettle plants in a gallon of water for a week, and apply the liquid to their plants as both a fertilizer and a pest repellent.

Some of this is folklore, some may be based on truth. It is known, however, that the plant's nitrogen-rich foliage decomposes into a humus as potent as manure. It is also true that a nettle sting is as painful as a bee sting, and the agony of a nettle sting can be reduced by rubbing the area with rhubarb or onion.

Choosing your vegetable plants is a matter of taste, and soil

We manage to grow vegetables in our heavy clay soil, but some are more challenging than others—sometimes for aesthetic reasons.

Carrots and parsnips, for example, prefer loose, sandy soil in which to extend their tap roots. In heavy clay, they'll send out a series of tentacles and you'll harvest plants that look more like an octopus than something you'd want to add to your casserole or salad. (Cathy refused to allow these repulsive creatures into the house, so we gave up on them.)

With an eye toward minimizing garden maintenance, here are our choices and suggestions:

Tomatoes—Many people consider any garden to be incomplete without at least a few tomato plants, and we tend to agree. We cultivate about eight plants each season, and they produce more than enough crop for eating fresh, making spaghetti and chili sauces, and handing out to friends and neighbours. To get maximum fruit from minimum space:

- Give them room. Tomatoes should be set about 3 feet apart.
- Keep them well watered, especially in hot weather, to prevent blossom-end rot. Tomatoes have shallow root systems and dry out quickly.
- Support the plants. Cages are popular, but they often need anchoring to hold the plants steadily when they're heavy with fruit. We like spiral stakes, which are sturdier.
- Remove suckers from the axis where side branches meet the main stem.
- Remove the lowest branches if they touch the ground.
- Work very generous amounts of compost into the soil before planting to sustain the plants through the growing season.
- Choose your varieties carefully. Nurseries have developed several tomato varieties that resist the most common diseases and identify them by code. If you have encountered certain diseases in the past, or know they can be a problem in your area, and are growing your tomato plants from seed, watch for these codes in the catalogues:
    V—Resistant to verticillium wilt
    F—Resistant to fusarium wilt
    L—Resistant to leaf spot
    T—Resistant to tobacco mosaic

We've had good success with these varieties in the past; the letters indicate their disease-resistant codes:

Big Beef (an All-America Selection)	V, F, T
Celebrity (an All-America Selection)	V, F, T
Park's Whopper (super-large beefsteak)	V, F, T
Roma (good Italian-type for freezing and sauces)	V, F
Floramerica (an All-America Selection)	V, F

All-America Selections and what they mean

Some of the tomatoes listed above, and a few vegetables below, are identified as "All-America Selections." The AAS designation is awarded to new flower and vegetable seeds that have been grown in trial gardens throughout the United States and Canada. Based on their performance and merit, the very best varieties are identified as "AAS," indicating they have proven themselves in most areas of the continent.

Beans—Bush beans are becoming a favourite thanks to their compact size and high production. We plant a row each spring, get several weeks of harvest in mid-summer, and add pole beans around the perimeters of some tomato cages for the plants to climb them. The pole beans start producing around the time the bush beans are finished, and we harvest beans through September.

Beets—This is an easy root crop to grow. We prefer them pickled, plus you can cook the greens and serve them like spinach.

Good varieties are Red Ace, Little Ball, Ruby Queen and Detroit Dark red.

Brussels sprouts—These are easier than cabbage and fun to grow, if you have a taste for them. If you are growing from seeds, start them indoors about a week before the last frost date and set the plants out in June. They'll really produce in cool fall weather. The best part of Brussels sprouts is that you can harvest them as needed. We've pulled sprouts from the plants in February, when they've been under a layer of snow!

Jade Cross is a good variety.

Cabbages—We grow two or three a year, if we have room. But cutworms, caterpillars and the need to ensure an even supply of water can make them tricky to grow properly.

If you want to try them, look for Savoy Ace, Red Haven and Copenhagen varieties.

Cauliflower and Broccoli—Two more high-maintenance vegetables. They grow best in cooler weather, have to be harvested at precisely the right time, and the cauliflower heads need to be protected from the sun. As if that's not enough, they're both favourite targets of insects, so the crop must be rotated regularly.

Corn—Yes, there's nothing like a fresh cob of corn directly from your garden into the pot. But be warned—growing a small plot of corn is more difficult than you may think. (See page 157.)

Cucumbers—We have two words of advice: Forget 'em. These plants are too susceptible to insects and disease to make them worthwhile,

---

The Secret Lives of Plants #9: Vintage Vegetables

- *Beets were widely cultivated around the time of Christ.*
- *Carrots were once all yellow or white varieties; orange carrots didn't become popular until the eighteenth century.*
- *Corn intrigued European settlers in North America, who found Native Americans growing it. When the settlers asked what the plant was, the Natives replied "maize," which meant "our life"— because corn sustained them more than any other food.*
- *Cucumbers were originally called "cowcumbers" presumably because they were used as cattle food.*
- *Peas were cultivated as far back as 7000 B.C.*
- *Radishes were so valued by the Greeks that gold ones were offered to the god Apollo.*
- *Lettuce was served cooked until the mid-nineteenth century.*
- *Tomatoes were grown during the early nineteenth century in purple and striped varieties. Some of these are still grown by heirloom gardeners who want to maintain these older types.*

—Dave & Cathy

---

in our opinion. For years we babied our cucumber plants, battled the beetles and worried over the wilt—and the result? Two or three miserable-looking cukes in September. Meanwhile, at our local farmer's market, we can purchase a bushel of fresh cucumbers for about five bucks at the height of the season. We'd rather leave these vegetables to the large-scale professional farmers.

Lettuce—Stick with leaf lettuce; it's far easier to grown than head lettuce, and you can harvest and eat the outer leaves all during the season.

Etna, Sierra and Summertime are all good varieties; we especially like Red Sail and New Red Fire for their crimson-tinged leaves.

Onions—Spanish onions are a trouble-free crop we enjoy growing. Hint: Bend or break the stalks from time to time and you'll force the plant to produce larger onions.

Kelsue Sweet and Giant Burgermaster Red are good varieties.

Peas—We plant only snap peas for salads and stir-fries. Pod peas are great when freshly picked and the sugar content is high, but frankly we have other things to do besides sitting under a tree and shelling a pot of peas.

Two good snap-pea varieties are Little Sweetie and Sugar Ann.

Peppers—Our kind of vegetable. Give them hot weather, decent soil and regular watering, and they'll produce a good crop. Plus, there are so many varieties to choose from. Two hints: Don't plant peppers in the same location where you grew tomatoes, potatoes or eggplant the previous year or two, because they're all susceptible to the same diseases; and don't water from overhead (i.e., with a sprinkler) because you will wash away pollen from the blossoms and produce no crop. Water from below with a soaker hose.

Suggested reliable varieties—Bell Boy, Jingle Bell (multiple miniature red fruit), Jackpot, Valencia (orange variety) and Redstart. For slightly spicier but not fiery hot, try Szentesi. Super Sweet Banana peppers are an interesting change.

Squash—These are fine vegetables to grow if you have the room. If you choose zucchini or other summer squash, one or two healthy plants should be enough to feed you, your family and several relatives. Winter squash do fine, but they will overrun your entire vegetable patch if not controlled (a good reason to choose acorn varieties in bush form). All squash love rich soil, so pour on the compost and manure in the spring.

A fresh idea for vegetables: A kitchen garden

We haven't tried this ourselves, but it sounds like an attractive alternative to planting a substantial—and high-maintenance— vegetable plot at the rear of your garden.

Unless you have a very large family or want to share your harvest with friends, you may get all the satisfaction you need from a small kitchen garden located just outside your back door. A plot as small as 5 feet square can produce plenty of tasty veggies through the summer.

Your choice of crops will be limited, of course—don't expect to harvest corn, potatoes or squash. But herbs and greens will be right at hand, and with a few touches your kitchen garden can be attractive to look at too.

Here's how to get started:

1. Remember the 6-hours-of-sunlight rule. Choose a location that delivers this much sunshine from May to September.

2. You're asking a lot from this plot of land, so spend some time in spring preparing it. Cover the entire area with compost or well-rotted manure to a depth of at least 2 to 3 inches. Till the soil about 8 inches deep, mixing the manure or compost well. Rake out any stones, roots, etc.

3. Outline your kitchen garden plot in flagstones, clay bricks or other edging material.

4. Group plants such as tomatoes (be sure to stake them), sweet peppers, leaf lettuce, radishes and bush beans—plus herbs such as rosemary, basil, thyme, parsley, sage and chives.

5. Mulch with cocoa bean hulls for an attractive appearance and pleasant aroma while inhibiting weeds and retaining soil moisture.

For zucchini, try Gold Rush and Cheffini. Other summer squash types we like are Early Whitebush and Sunburst; these are scallop-types with a pleasant mild and moist texture.

For winter squash, consider Table King and Table Gold. Both are acorn bush–types, so they'll take up less room. If you have enough room, you might consider spreaders such as Ultra Butternut and Butterbush.

Turnip—Now and then we plant turnips, and at the end of the season we're still not sure why. They're not difficult to grow, although they don't care for hot weather. But in our heavy clay soil they have problems forming a normal shape, and the ones we harvest resemble pregnant carrots—not an appetizing sight.

Entire books have been written on growing vegetables in a home garden. Since the theme of this book has been to reduce garden maintenance—and most vegetables are anything but low-maintenance—we haven't done more than touch on the topic here.

And on the seventh day, the racoons feasted

One year we decided to grow sweet corn in our garden. Hey, if we can raise 6-foot delphiniums and precious begonias, corn should be a walk in the park.

Sure—New York's Central Park, on a dark night.

The corn grew beautifully, and soon the word spread among our neighbours—the ones with ringed tails and black circles around their eyes.

We have racoons. You have racoons. Everyone reading this book has racoons. Racoons are the Revenue Canada agents and undertakers of the animal world, and they'll get you in the end no matter what you do.

The day following the First Night of the Racoons, we did some investigating. We're basically Live And Let Live kind of people, so we looked for a passive way of deterring these midnight bandits from our tender corn.

"Newspapers," somebody told us. "Spread 'em around the plants. The 'coons hate the noise they make."

So we spread fresh newspapers every morning. And it worked. For five nights. On the sixth night, the raccoons read Dear Abby while nibbling on our precious corn kernels.

"Music," somebody else suggested. "Leave a radio playing all night. Spooks the heck out of 'em."

So we ran an extension cord from the house to the corn patch, plugged in a radio/tape player tuned to an all-night rock station, and went to sleep. (Dave wanted to set the tape deck playing an endless Barry Manilow cassette from dusk to dawn, but we feared being charged with excessive cruelty to animals . . .)

It worked for five nights. On the sixth morning, we found well-chewed cobs of corn near the Sony.

"They don't like light," somebody offered. "Shine a spotlight on the garden to scare them away." The next night, 100 watts of incandescent power shone down upon our struggling corn patch. Success! For five nights.

On the sixth morning, we got the impression that the racoons had a midnight picnic, dancing to the music and checking their stock market investments in the newspaper while eating our corn.

"It's people they can't stand," we heard next. "Leave some old clothes in the garden and they'll think you're in there!"

So Dave deposited sweaty items of clothing among the corn rows. The vegetable garden reeked like a college locker room in mid-summer.

You guessed it. The sweaty clothes strategy worked for five nights. By the sixth, the 'coons were using Dave's clothing for bibs while they devoured the corn.

"You need drastic action," someone finally suggested.

"How drastic?" we asked. "Shotguns scare us."

"Not shotguns," we were told. "An electric fence. Put some chicken wire on wooden stakes, hook it up to a low-voltage transformer, plug it in, and the racoons are gone." Now our corn patch looked like Stalag 17. Spotlights, electrified fences, dirty laundry —if Amnesty International saw our garden, we'd be accused of running a gulag!

But it worked. Kind of.

If the earth beneath the wire was too dry, the circuit wouldn't connect, the racoons felt nothing, and dinner was served. If any plants touched the chicken wire, they would ground the circuit, with no effect on the raiding racoons.

At the end of the season we harvested perhaps two dozen cobs of corn. Our enjoyment was dulled by the realization that each cob cost us about ten bucks to raise. After daily newspapers, all-night radio, midnight sunshine, discarded sweatshirts and an electrified enclosure, the racoons won anyway.

All but one. During the electric fence technique, we found him dead the next morning, touching the live wire.

We were mortified, of course. Until Dave, surveying the newspapers, radio, lights and clothing, said: "Look on the bright side. Maybe he died laughing at us."

Maybe he did.

—Cathy

CHAPTER 11

THE JOYS OF STARTING FROM SCRATCH

Each year in May, we hold a plant sale at our home. The tradition began modestly a few years ago as a way of disposing of extra plants grown by Dave over the winter. Obviously, we're doing a lot of things right, because local gardeners seem to look forward to our sale, and we're often cleared out of stock by Sunday.

We're not interested in turning our hobby into a profession—it wouldn't be as much fun if we did—so we don't mind if you become as adept at raising your plants from seeds as we are.

Selecting young plants from nurseries is easier than growing your own. But an entire dimension to gardening can only be explored when you're there at the actual birth and delivery of the little green creatures. On a more practical note, you'll hasten the growing season, save yourself some money and be the first in your neighbourhood with interesting new plant varieties that are not—nor may ever be—available from the local plant nursery. These include, for example, some of the new All-America Selections each year.

For us Canadians, there's another benefit:

On cold, bleak February days when it seems spring will never return again, the sight of new green seedlings emerging from the planting beds in your basement can be very reassuring. It doesn't quite measure up to a week on a beach in Mexico, but it's a darn sight cheaper and more convenient!

Read this warning before proceeding

*Propagating your own plants can lead to a serious and often debili-
tating disorder with no known cure. I must be frank: I suffer from
a severe case, and the condition is, to my knowledge, incurable.*

*The disorder is marked by compulsive behaviour to grow plants
from seeds in ever-increasing numbers, and in an ever-widening
range of species and varieties. It can lead to serious problems
such as growing far too many plants to be accommodated in one's
garden, and neglecting important events such as breakfast in
order to rush downstairs (to the seedling nursery) or outside
(to the greenhouse) to inspect the emergence and progress of
seedlings.*

*I have heard the disorder described using a number of terms,
from the clinical Excessive Horticultural-Germination Syndrome
to Cathy's description ("Dave's at it again!").*

*There is no known cure. Goodness knows, Cathy has done her
best to cure me. She has hidden seed catalogues from my sight,
and founded a local branch of Propagators Anonymous. Nothing
seems to work.*

*So be warned. Information contained in this chapter can be
highly contagious and severely debilitating to other aspects of life.
It is, however, rarely fatal.*

—Dave

Here's our guide to growing seedlings, with an eye to minimizing time,
money and effort:

Lighting: Adjustable fluorescents do the trick

You can start with a few boxes of seeds on a windowsill, but for more
convenience and more seedlings, invest a few dollars in a fluorescent
light fixture. Nothing too elaborate is needed here. Hanging fluorescent
fixtures are inexpensive—perhaps $25 to $35 each, and you'll save that
much the first year. Choose fixtures with 48-inch tubes and a reflector.

If necessary, equip the fixture with a plug (if you want to use an inexpensive automatic timing device), and a mix of warm-white and cool-white tubes. (The special "Grow Lights" are more expensive and unnecessary if you use an even mix of warm and cool.)

You will need either a means of raising and lowering the light, or an adjustable shelf for your seedling trays. Use a security timer—the kind you use to turn your home lights on and off when you're on vacation—plugged into an outlet. Connect the fixture with the timer to provide the required hours of light per day—usually 14 to 16 hours—for your seedlings.

Soil: Keep it sterile

You may be tempted to start your seedlings in soil taken directly from your garden. Please—don't even think about it! Insect and disease microbes that can be tolerated in your garden can create havoc and misery among your new seedlings.

If you're starting on a small scale, purchase good-quality sterilized soil mix from your garden supply dealer. When you need larger quantities of seeding soil, it may be time to mix your own and save a little money. All seeding soils consist of peat moss, vermiculite and perlite. We use one measure of peat moss, one and a half measures of vermiculite and a half measure of perlite.

While this mixture works well to get seedlings started, it tends to dry out faster than common garden soil. If you can obtain good sterile bags of soil, add about one measure to the above recipe to extend the time between watering periods.

Containers: Pay your money and take your choice

The very best containers for growing seedlings are made from peat mixtures or fibre materials. Besides permitting the plant to breathe, they are also sterile. Unfortunately they're also the most expensive choice, and cannot be recycled.

Almost any container of suitable size will do, from styrofoam cups (perfect for starting geraniums) and restaurant take-out containers, to recycled plastic flats and cell packs from garden nurseries. They should be at least 2 to 3 inches deep. You'll need to add drainage holes.

A candle, a nail and a pair of pliers do the best job here. Holding the nail with the pliers, heat the tip in the candle flame and melt three or four holes in the plastic base. (It's not necessary to heat the nail for styrofoam containers.)

Whichever you choose, be sure to sterilize them thoroughly. For the most part, we use recycled containers obtained from friends and neighbours. Before using, we wash them thoroughly in a mixture of soap, bleach and hot water.

"No, it's not a legal holiday from school"

When our children were small, I managed to recruit free help in performing a day-long chore, thanks to some inspiration from Tom Sawyer and a little hype.

I spread the word through the neighbourhood that the weekend of the Great Pot-Wash was coming up, so all the local kids had better get ready!

That weekend, I gathered all the young volunteers in our garden, said a few phrases in gibberish over the garden hose, and announced the ritual: We were going to wash pots, which would please the Great Green God.

Hey, it worked! With much gusto, kids would start washing old soil from used planting pots. Of course, it would eventually break down into water fights with the garden hose. And I didn't have too many repeat visitors the next year. But, for a while, we had an interesting warm-weather ritual: our family got to meet most of the kids in the area and I even got quite a few pots clean for recycling.

—Dave

Getting started: Avoid the deadly "damping off"

Fill your clean, dry and sterile containers with soil mixture and moisten completely—the soil should be wet but not soggy.

At this point, take steps to avoid the problem of "damping off." This fungus disease is a major source of discouragement to first-time seedling growers. It develops on the surface of the growing medium (i.e., the planting soil) and causes the seedlings to wilt and rot. One day your new baby plants are green and perky, and the next day they're ready for the compost heap.

It's all very upsetting, but fortunately you have three effective ways of preventing it.

> • Apply a product called No-Damp to your seedling beds as directed; it's available at most garden-supply shops. Or
> • Add a thin layer of vermiculite, milled sphagnum moss (also known as "No Damp-Off") to the surface after planting the seeds. Or
> • Add a mixture of the two—my favourite—to the surface after planting.

Soil that's not soil, and other mysteries

All seeds grow in soil—except the ones you start yourself.

Sterile, soil-less mixtures provide seeds with an advantage over their cousins in the wild. Free of insects and disease, a proper soil-less mixture also drains well, yet holds sufficient moisture for the plant to develop. A better term than "soil" is "medium," consisting of several ingredients.

Peat moss is made from dry, decomposed aquatic plants. While it is excellent at holding moisture, it has little or no nutrition for plants.

Sphagnum moss is harvested green from bogs, then dried. It is fairly sterile, light in weight and can absorb up to 20 times its weight in water. For seeding purposes, it must be shredded first. Sphagnum has very little food value, and is highly acidic.

Perlite, ground from volcanic ash, does not hold water but suspends it on the surface. The grey-white material contains no plant nutrients but is light and sterile and provides aeration.

Vermiculite, unlike perlite, can hold large amounts of water, is light and sterile, and is neutral—neither acidic nor alkaline. Made of expanded mica, the material is high in magnesium and potassium.

Sand and garden soil are filled with microbes, may be lean in nutrients and are generally unsuitable for ideal germination. Avoid them.

Choosing your seeds: Be picky, picky, picky

Forget bargain seeds, if you encounter any. They're no bargain at all. Purchase your seeds from a reliable source, and look for a guarantee that the seeds are true to both their species and variety, free of disease and fresh to ensure high levels of germination.

Collecting seeds from your own plants and other sources can be fun, but often the plants you obtain will not be identical to their parents thanks to tricks such as cross-pollination. Germination is also variable because the success level will depend on things such as the level of maturity, processing and storage of the seeds.

The majority of seeds—especially annuals and vegetables—will retain their viability for several years if stored under the right conditions. Once your seed package has been opened, place any unused seeds in a clean, dry airtight container and keep in a cool, dark place. (Yes, your refrigerator is perfect.)

The life of seeds varies widely, according to the mother plant. Parsnips, parsley, onions and delphiniums are rarely viable beyond the first year. Yet we have had fine success with fifteen-year-old seeds from broccoli, cauliflower and tomatoes. From time to time, newscasts carry reports of seeds estimated to be thousands of years old retaining their viability and germinating into fresh, new plants. Amazing little things, aren't they?

In the beginning: Grow what you know

When starting out, choose seeds from plants that are likely to be successful the first time. They'll give you confidence in your ability and avoid some of the problems you might encounter with some cranky plant species.

Here are some popular, easy-to-grow plants worth considering, along with the estimated time to leave between seeding and moving out to your garden, with the plants requiring the longest lead-time listed first:

Pansy	15 weeks
Dusty Miller	12 weeks
Salvia	12 weeks
Dianthus (Pinks)	12 weeks
Alyssum	8 to 9 weeks
Marigolds	8 to 9 weeks
Cosmos	7 to 8 weeks
Peppers	7 to 8 weeks
Tomatoes	6 weeks
Cabbage	4 to 5 weeks
Cauliflower	4 to 5 weeks

Broccoli	4 to 5 weeks
Brussels Sprouts	4 to 5 weeks
Zinnia elegans	Don't start too early—they need only two to three weeks before setting out, and will actually start to deteriorate if kept in cell packs any longer.

Special treatment: Some seeds require a little encouragement

While most annuals (including vegetables) can be started from seeds directly out of the package, some perennials require coaxing. If your seed supplier recommends scarification, soaking or stratification, here's how to do it:

Scarification—Seeds with extra-hard shells need this treatment to help germination. For plants such as mallow (*Hibiscus* species) and Lupin (*Lupinus* species), nick the seed casings with a sharp knife, file or sandpaper.

Soaking—Smaller hard-shelled seeds, such as sweet pea (*Lathyrus odoratus*), parsley and morning glory (*Ipomoea purpurea*) can be soaked overnight in a hot water bath. Better still, fold the seeds in some paper towelling, soak in hot water and slide seeds and wet towel into a plastic bag to retain moisture. The next day, drain the water and plant the seeds immediately without drying.

Stratification—This involves submitting seeds to cold temperatures, inducing them out of dormancy. It can be achieved by soaking the seeds in water for 24 hours, placing them in a plastic bag containing a mixture of moist peat moss and sand, and leaving the bag in your refrigerator, at a temperature of 1 to 5°C (34 to 41°F) for 4 to 12 weeks. Some seeds require colder temperatures, which means time spent in your freezer compartment. Check your seed supplier for details.

Handling small seeds: Whatever you do, don't sneeze!

Not all plants spring from seeds as large as those from sunflowers, tomatoes or even poppies. Consider petunias and begonias, for example. One ounce of Olympia fibrous begonia seeds contains 2,000,000—that's two million—individual specks (which, by the way, costs over $11,000 if you were buying these particular seeds by weight.)

Forget about handling these tiny dust-sized seeds with your fingers. I use this method:

First I spread the seeds on a sheet of pure white paper. Then I cut lengths of cotton thread to match the width of my planting container. Then, after moistening the thread in my mouth, I lower it to the seeds until ten or twelve of the little devils cling to it, and carefully place the seeds and thread in the planting medium.

For seeds slightly larger, but still too small to handle by hand, use the moistened head of a small nail to lift and plant individual seeds.

Those without patience to treat seeds in this manner can simply pour them from the package and thin the seedlings out later. Aside from wasting seeds, this can become tedious on its own, especially at transplanting time.

Seeding: Trust the seed producer, and don't trust your memory

Before planting your seeds, read the back of the seed package or the information that arrived with the seeds, and follow the instructions exactly.

Not all seeds achieve ideal germination under the same conditions. Most require planting in a moist soil medium to a depth roughly equal to their own diameter. Some smaller seeds need light to start germinating, so they shouldn't be covered at all. Others germinate in total darkness.

Light needs of some common seeds:

Need light: Ageratum, celocia, coleus, dusty miller, impatiens, Oriental poppy, snapdragon.

Need darkness: Calendula, forget-me-not, nasturtium, pansy, periwinkle, sweet pea.

Don't really care: Alyssum, cosmos, marigold, zinnia.

For others, consult the seed package or instructions from the seed grower.

With the seeds in place, label the containers carefully. Trusting your memory to recall the species and variety of each group of seedlings is a risk not worth taking. We make a point of identifying them all on labels, using a chart to record the date the seeds were planted, how many seeds were sown and the number of seeds that germinated, along with the date of their appearance.

Slide the entire container into a clear plastic bag and set it either near a window (not in direct sunlight) or beneath the fluorescent lights (except for seeds that require darkness for germination). For most seeds, temperatures between 20 and 25°C (68 to 75°F) are ideal—check the seed producer's guidelines for the ideal temperature range.

For temperatures of 21°C (70°F) or higher, placing the seed container on top of your refrigerator (if it's warm up there) or on the ballast of your fluorescent lamp will provide bottom heat to improve germination levels and produce stronger seedlings. This latter choice works very well for us. Another method: Wire two lightbulb sockets inside a wooden box and install low-wattage (15 watt) incandescent bulbs. (You might line the interior with heavy tin foil for extra heat and a margin of safety.) Set a thin sheet of metal on top to support the seedling containers and plug it in.

Finally, many garden supply dealers sell heating cable that can be adapted for bottom-heaters as well.

When the plants germinate, remove them immediately from the plastic bag and set under the fluorescent lights, within an inch of the tubes. Watch the soil—when it begins to dry out, immerse the entire container in a tray of water at room temperature or warmer, permitting the water to seep up into the soil medium and not disturb the seedling roots, then replace under the lights.

Transplanting: Gently does it

When the seedlings have developed four true leaves, it's time to thin them out and transplant them. Decide how many you want to transplant and fill a sufficient number of suitable containers with the soil medium. Moisten the medium thoroughly with a water-soluble transplant fertilizer—10-52-10.

Using a pocket knife or similar tool, separate the seedlings, lift them gently and, after using the knife blade to open the transplant soil sufficiently, lower them in place. Pat the soil around the seedlings and replace the container under the lights.

Keep the seedlings moist and fed with suitable water-soluble fertilizer (I use 12-36-12 for flowering plants and vegetables), but mix at about one third the strength recommended by the fertilizer manufacturer. Apply this mixture each time you water the plants.

Hardening off and moving out

Until now, the young plants have been coddled indoors, so it's necessary to acquaint them to the real world over time.

This is called "hardening off," a week-long period of adjustment for the plants. Set them out each morning in a sheltered area of the garden, on a table or other elevated device to foil slugs, and move the plants inside at night. After 2 or 3 days, provide them with direct sunlight for half a day, increasing their exposure to direct sun gradually for the rest of the 7-day period. Keep them well watered each day.

After the risk of frost has passed the plants are ready for transplanting to their permanent residence.

Reduce transplant shock by disturbing the roots as little as possible. Deep-set vegetables such as eggplant, tomatoes, leeks, sweet peppers, cabbages, cucumbers, melons and zucchini should be planted right up to their first set of leaves.

Water deeply, at least once a week. Try to water only in early mornings, to avoid leaving the foliage wet through the night—a great opportunity for disease to develop.

Fertilizing is a matter of choice—do you prefer a healthy mix of compost in the soil (our personal favourite), a slow-release dry fertilizer or a regular feeding of water-soluble plant food? If you choose either of the last two, make certain the middle number—phosphorus—is at least twice as high as the other numbers (nitrogen and potash). For example: 5-10-5 for slow release dry fertilizer, or 15-30-15 for some water-soluble formulas. Whatever you do, avoid the 7-7-7 fertilizer used on lawns. Your seedlings need root, flower or fruit development, and that's a job for the phosphorus portion of the mix.

Secrets of the cold frame

Starting your own seedlings is an obvious way of getting an early start for annuals and many frost-sensitive vegetables. Combine this with a cold frame, and you could be enjoying blooms and veggies several weeks ahead of your neighbours. In many regions of Canada, it can also extend the growing season well into November.

A cold frame is simply an open box with a removable glass cover, set in a well-drained sunny location of your garden. During the day, the cold frame traps heat from the sun, encouraging growth. At night, the frame retains sufficient heat to prevent damage from spring frost.

The depth of the box should be about 18 inches at its highest point, and the length and width can be as large as practical. Actually, most gardeners choose a discarded wood-framed window (with glass intact, of course) as the cold frame cover, using the window's dimensions to dictate the size of their cold frame. The window should overlap the top of the box, preventing heat from escaping.

Almost any kind of scrap lumber will do, but it's best to avoid pressure-treated wood—cedar is ideal. Small brass angle supports are all that's needed to hold the wood in place. Slope the height of the box down to about 15 inches to permit snow and water to drain away.

Install the cold frame securely into the ground, burying the sides about 6 inches deep and facing south. Remove the soil inside the frame and replace with a mix of soil, compost and manure in roughly equal quantities. Give the seedlings a good start here until the risk of frost has passed, and move them to their permanent location.

Oh, the joys of living with a seed-propagation addict!

Dave thinks becoming wrapped up in starting your own seedlings is like catching a disease. I'd call it more like acquiring an addiction.

Living with an addict of any kind can be trying. One year, Dave decided to save some money on sterile soil for his seedlings by making his own. I returned home to be almost overwhelmed by a horrible smell all through the house. Holding my nose, I traced it to our kitchen. In fact, it seemed to be coming from our oven! Sure enough, the oven was on, with the temperature set at 200°F. But what was that granular brown substance inside— the source of the stench?

Of course. Dave was attempting his own soil sterilization.

It seemed like a good idea at the time, I must admit. But trust me: don't try it, unless you enjoy the prospect of fumigating your kitchen afterward.

—Cathy

CHAPTER 12

THE MORE YOU GIVE, THE MORE YOU GET

We began this book with the idea of helping you obtain maximum enjoyment with minimum toil from your garden. It was never our intention to suggest methods of totally avoiding work in your garden, even if we knew how. The rewards of gardening are like every reward in life—the satisfaction you receive from it is in direct proportion to the effort you invest in it.

We were most interested in providing you with the opportunity to demonstrate your creativity, not your physical stamina. A sculptor, for example, should be able to focus all attention on carving the stone and leave the quarry work to others. If we have managed to help you reduce the "quarry work" in your garden—routine weeding, trimming, cultivating, feeding and so on—we've kept our promise to ourselves and you.

Among the most tiresome chores of gardening is fall clean-up. Now that we've dealt with low-maintenance plants—perennials, trees, shrubs and ground cover—we can even suggest specific ways of cutting this particular task to a minimum.

Here are our suggestions for reducing time and energy for fall clean-up. Some you can apply right away; others will depend on your selection of plants and application of previous ideas (remember mulch! mulch! mulch!) during the growing season. But all are effective, to one degree or another. Taken together, you'll find more time on your hands to relax or maybe even make your garden larger and more complex without demanding more of your time.

• Try to create a self-maintaining garden by reducing any plants that produce litter.

• Maximize ground cover, especially evergreen species.

• When planting deciduous trees and shrubs, locate them separately from any lawn areas. Set them among ground covers or blanket the surrounding area with organic mulches. Let the leaves remain where they fall, and permit nature to take its course. Ground covers and organic mulches will absorb the leaves, improving the soil naturally.

Things to do when the show is over

Most people love fall in our corner of the world, although it may be a more bittersweet time for gardeners than for most. After all, fall brings a double whammy: Your show of blooms is over, and there are always chores to be done.

We assembled a few suggestions to reduce fall chores, and added some low-effort ideas that should cut your work the following spring. Here they are:

• Be sure to continue watering through any dry spells during the fall season. It will strengthen your perennials and ensure better plants next spring.

• Watch moisture levels from rain or early snow. If you encounter a dry autumn, water trees and shrubs thoroughly before winter sets in. This is an important step in helping them survive to spring with minimal damage.

• Walk among your perennials, working in a little bone meal around the plants to help build their root systems. This isn't really essential for healthy plants, so don't fret if you miss doing it. But it does give your plants an extra boost and is a good idea if you have the time.

• After the first killing frost, toss the dead annuals on the compost, empty the containers, remove the soil and invert the pots to prevent damage over winter.

• Don't bother raking leaves from your vegetable garden. Till them into the soil in the spring.

• Unless they're in large, unsightly clumps, why bother raking leaves from deep within your perennial garden? By mid-spring next year they'll be adding to the organic content of your soil, hidden behind new shoots from your perennials and shrubs. We say, Leave 'em be.

• Leaf blowers and vacuums are noisy little devils, we admit, and we don't approve of them being used when a good push broom does a quieter job. But they are real work-savers for removing fallen leaves from places where we would rather not have them.

• Postpone raking the lawn as much as possible by attaching a grass catcher to your lawn mower. Be certain to remove leaves from the lawn before the snow flies, and make your final grass cut of the season a little shorter than usual.

• For fall clean-up of perennials, check our suggestions at the end of Chapter Eight.

• Try to keep large flower seed heads around for the birds. Nothing brightens a garden in winter than the sight of jays, cardinals and chickadees feeding on seeds from the previous summer.

• When winter arrives, resist the urge to spread salt on walks adjacent to your flower beds—it can cause serious damage. Try using sand instead.

It's an art and a science

The joy and the frustration of gardening both come from the same source: the unpredictability of it all.

In many ways, you are only a small element in the success of your garden. No matter how attentive you may be in your gardening activities, many events remain beyond your control, and all you can do is react in the best way you know. Will the coming growing season be exceptionally warm or cold, with substantially more or less average rainfall? Will garden pests ranging from scale to caterpillars be virtually undetectable all season long, or will there be a plague from May to the first frost? Each spring, we take the year's first step into the garden unaware of all that is about to unfold with the weather, with pests . . . and even with the flowers we're anxious to tend.

Here's a good example:

One season, we planted a clump of nine purple coneflowers in a corner of our garden. All the plants were healthy and identical when we put them in the ground, and all received the same care and attention. But only seven made it through the season. Two simply gave up. If they were students, you might expect two out of nine to fail the year through lack of study, reduced ability or just goofing off. But these were identical plants. They should have performed identically, but they didn't. We still don't know why.

Do things like that discourage us? Not in the least. Like life itself, the stubbornly independent coneflowers were unpredictable and mystifying.

And that—along with the beauty we enjoy and the lessons that it teaches us—is why we love gardening so much.

We bet it's your reason as well.

Guess what I got you at the auction, dear?

To people like us, gardening is a passion. Not an all-consuming passion, perhaps, but one that manages to influence more corners of our lives than we expected.

Folks who don't share this passion have difficulty fully understanding it, and a few of the things we do without a second thought strike them as . . . well, as a little weird sometimes.

For example: Dave took a week's vacation a few years ago and travelled with a group of old buddies from high school, driving deep into the United States to visit a friend who lives there. The day before returning home, Dave and his buddies went shopping for souvenirs for their wives. The other guys chose perfume, jewellery and similar gifts. Dave chose something for me too:

A set of Japanese beetle traps.

Hey, they were a fine gift. Couldn't get this type in Canada.

A few years later, I attended a charity auction, determined to select something for Dave. There was much to choose from and bid on, but I made my decision quickly. I bid and won, at a much lower price than I expected to pay. Obviously, few people recognized the true value of the item.

"I got you something," I announced to Dave when I returned home. "It'll be here tomorrow, and you'll love it!"

As promised, the gift was delivered on time, arriving in the back of a truck that deposited its contents in the driveway:

A ton of well-rotted manure.

I was right—Dave loved it. He spent the day carrying it in a wheelbarrow back to the flower beds, wearing a big grin on his face.

Passionate gardeners understand completely. The rest of you can smile, if you like.

—Cathy

Your Personal Rusty Rake List of Favourites

SELECTED FOR LOW-MAINTENANCE AND HIGH REWARDS.

	Common name	Latin

Easy-care perennials:

Special selections:
(Prima Donnas,
Gentle Giants, etc.)

Selected shrubs:

Tolerable trees:

Veggies:

Ground covers:

INDEX

A

Abies concolor (*see* fir, white)
Abutilon (*see* flowering maple)
Acer ginnala (*see* maple, amur)
Acer palmatum (*see* maple, Japanese)
acidity (pH levels) 52
Aconitum napellus (*see* monkshood)
Actinidia kolomikta (*see* kiwi vine)
Aegopodium podagraria (*see* goutweed)
Ageratum (*Ageratum houstonianum*) 136
Ajuga *reptans* 89,125
Akebia quinata (*see* five-leaf Akebia)
Alcea rosea (*see* hollyhock)
Alchemilla mollis (*see* lady's mantle)
All-America Selections 152
Allium giganteum (*see* onions, ornamental)
Amelanchier arborea (*see* downy serviceberry)
anemone 125, 126
annuals
    as high-maintenance plants 11
    characteristics 135
    colours 41
    expense, maintenance 40
    feeding 62
    in containers 36, 37
    low-maintenance 136, 137
    self-sowing 41
Antirrhinum majus (*see* snapdragon)
Aquilegia (*see* columbine)
arborists 118
Aruncus dioicus (*see* goat's beard)
Artemesia ludoviciana (*see* silver sage)
Astilbe 11, 43, 125, 130
Athyrium niponicum (*see* Japanese painted fern)
Austrian pine (*Pinus nigra*) 64
autumn 171, 172

B

baby's breath (*Gypsophila*) 125
bacopa 145
basil 145, 148, 155
beans 152
beauty bush (*Kolkwitzia amabilis*) 105
beets 152
begonias, fibrous 136, 143
Bergenia cordifolia (*see* elephant ears)
Betula papyrifera (*see* birch tree)
biennials 139
birch leaf miner 64
birch tree (*Betula Papyrifera*) 13

bird feeders 28
bird's nest spruce (*Picea abies* 'Nidiformis') 85,113
birds as pest control 66, 69
black spot 37
black-eyed Susan (*Rudbeckia fulgida*) 121
blanket flower (*Gaillardia*) 11, 125
blazing star (*Liatris*) 125
bleeding heart (*Dicentra spectabilis*) 11, 43, 125, 128
blue-mist shrub (*Caryopteris* x *clandonensis*) 105
Bonsai-style pruning 30
'borrowed views' 26
brussels sprouts 152
bucket apron 80
Buddleia davidii (*see* butterfly bush)
bugbane (*Cimicifuga*) 125
bugleweed (*Ajuga*) 89,125
burning bush (*Euonymous alatus*) 105
butterfly bush (*Buddleia davidii*) 105

C

cabbage 153
Calamagrostis x *acutiflora* (*see* ornamental grasses)
Campanula medium (*see* Canterbury bells)
canna lilies 142
Canterbury bells (*Campanula medium*) 128, 139
Caragana arborescens (*see* Siberian pea-shrub)
carrots 151
Caryopteris x *clandonensis* (*see* blue-mist shrub)
Catharanthus rosea (*see* vinca)
cauliflower and broccoli 153
celosia—wheat (*Celosia spicata*) 139
Celosia argentea plumosa (*see* cockscomb)
Cerastium (*see* snow-in-summer)
Cercidiphyllum japonicum (*see* Katsura tree)
Chamaecyparis nootkatensis (*see* Nootka false cypress)
Chelone obliqua (*see* turtlehead)
chemical fertilizers 61
chives 145, 148, 149, 155
Christmas rose (*Helleborus niger*) 125, 126
Chrysanthemum vulgare (*see* tansy)
Cimicifuga (*see* bugbane *Cimicifuga*)
clematis 8, 110, 111, 112
Cleome spinosa (*see* spider flower)
Clethra alnifolia (*see* summersweet clethra)

cockscomb plume (*Celosia argentea plumosa*) 137

coleus (*Coleus blumei*) 136, 143

columbine (*Aquilegia*) 125

compost 33, 55, 56, 57, 58, 61

composters 55

container plants 145

containers 40, 41, 62, 66, 112, 115, 135, 142, 144, 145, 167, 171

  planting 143

  types 144

Convallaria (*see* lily-of-the-valley)

coral bells

  (*Heuchera micrantha* 'Palace Purple') 122

  (*Heuchera sanguinea*) 9

Coreopsis verticillata (*see* tickseed)

corkscrew Hazel (*Corylus avellana* 'Contorta') 27, 107

corn 153

corncobs 57

Corylus avellana 'Contorta' (*see* corkscrew Hazel)

cosmos (*Cosmos bipinnatus*) 136

Cornus (*see* dogwood)

Cortaderia selloana (*see* grasses—ornamental)

cotoneasters (*C. horizontalis, C. dammeri*) 90

crab-apple trees 65

cranesbill (*see* geranium: perennial)

cucumbers 153

D

dahlberg daisies 145

dahlias 142

daphne (*Daphne* x *burkwoodii*) 107

day lilies (*Hemerocallis*) 86, 90, 122, 125

dead nettle (*Lamium*) 43

deadheading 15

delphinium (*D. elatum*) 35, 41, 82, 125, 128, 164

Dianthus barbatus (*see* sweet William)

Dicentra spectabilis (*see* bleeding heart)

Dictamnus albus (*see* gas plant)

Digitalis (*see* foxglove)

dill 49

dogwood

  kousa (*Cornus kousa*) 115

  pagoda (*Cornus alternifolia*) 115

downy serviceberry (*Amelanchier arborea*) 114

dusty miller 136, 143

E

earwigs 69

Easter lilies (*Lillium Longiflorum*) 141

easy-going annuals (*see* "Annuals: low maintenance")

Echinacea purpurea (*see* purple coneflower)

edging 79

elephant ears (*Bergenia cordifolia*) 122

Elymus arenarius 'Glaucus' (*see* ornamental grasses)

English Ivy (*Hedera helix*) 43, 90

euonymous, winter creeper (*Euonymous fortunei*) 92, 113

Euonymous alatus (*see* burning bush)

Eupatorium maculatum (*see* Joe Pye weed)

Euphorbia (*see* spurge)

European beech (*Fagus sylvatica* 'Purpurea Tricolor') 114

evergreens

  "candles" (new growth) 113

  choosing 112, 113

  general 27, 37

F

fall clean-up 170

Fagus sylvatica 'Purpurea Tricolor' (*see* European beech)

false sunflower (*Heliopsis helianthoides*) 127

fan-flower (*Scaevola*) 145

featherleaf rodgersia (*Rodgersia pinnata* 'Elegans') 124

Festuca glauca (*see* ornamental grasses)

fir, white (*Abies concolor*) 113

five-leaf Akebia (*Akebia quinata*) 111

fleeceflower (*Polygonum affine*) 89, 90

flower beds

  planning 32

  size 10

flowering maple (*Abutilon*) 145

flowers in vegetable beds 149

forget-me-not (*Myosotis sylvatica*) 139

forsythia 15

foxglove (*Digitalis*) 129, 139

fruit trees 17

G

Gaillardia (*see* blanket flower)

Galium odoratum (*see* sweet woodruff)

gardens

  environment 29

  formal and informal 20

  four-season areas 28

  mixing colours in 138

  new and existing 22

  planning 3, 22, 29, 32

  preparing beds 132

  rural and city 20

  shady and sunny 21

  "surprises" 45

garden sheds 28, 45

garden tours 12

gas plant (*Dictamnus albus*) 125, 129

geranium

  annual (*Pelargonium*) 136, 145

  perennial 190, 122, 125

Ginkgo biloba (*see* maidenhair tree)

gladiola 38, 142

gloriosa daisy (*Rudbeckia hirta* 'Indian Summer') 136, 137, 139
gloves 79
goat's beard (*Aruncus dioicus*) 123, 125
goutweed (*Aegopodium podagraria* 'Variegatum') 90
grass clippings 57
grasses—ornamental 28, 46, 92, 93, 94
  blue fescue (*Festuca glauca*) 96
  blue lyme grass (*Elymus arenarius* 'Glaucus') 95, 96
  blue oat grass (*Helictotrichon sempervirens*) 96
  control of invasive types 95
  favourites 96, 97
  feather reed grass (*Calamagrostis x acutiflora* 'Karl Foerster') 96
  fountain grass (*Pennisetum alopecuroides*) 96
  feeding 95
  Japanese blood grass (*Imperata cylindrica* 'Rubra') 96
  maiden grass—variegated (*Miscanthus sinensis* 'Morning Light') 97
  maintenance 37
  pampas grass (*Cortaderia selloana*) 96
  purple moor grass (*Molinia caerulea* 'Variegata') 95, 97
  red fountain grass (*Pennisetum setaceum* 'Rubrum') 97
  ribbon grass (*Phalaris arundinacea*—picta) 95, 97
  sarabande silver grass (*Miscanthus Sinensis* 'Sarabande') 96
  selection 93
  switch grass (*Panicum virgatum* 'Squaw') 97
  zebra grass (*Miscanthus sinensis* 'Zebrinus') 97
ground cover 86, 88, 89, 100
Gypsophila (*see* baby's breath)

H
Hamamelis vernalis (*see* witchhazel, vernal)
hardiness zones 25
Harry Lauder's Walking Stick (*see* Corkscrew Hazel)
hawthorn 65
Hedera helix (*see* English ivy)
hedges 2, 14, 15, 20, 21, 36, 39, 40, 43, 100
Helichrysum (*see* licorice plant)
Helictotrichon sempervirens (*see* ornamental grasses)
Heliopsis helianthoides (*see* false sunflower)
Helleborus niger (*see* Christmas rose)
Hemerocallis (*see* day lilies)
herbicides 64
Heuchera (*see* coral bells)
Hibiscus (*see* rose mallow)
Hibiscus syriacus (*see* rose-of-Sharon)
hollyhock (*Alcea rosea*) 77, 139

hornets 70
hosta 11, 43, 65, 88, 92, 125, 130, 131
honeysuckle, climbing (*Lonicera x brownii* 'Dropmore Scarlet') 111
hydrangea, Annabell (*Hydrangea arborescens*) 41, 105
hydrangea, climbing (*Hydrangea anomala*—petiolaris) 111
Hypericum prolificum (*see* St. John's wort)

I
impatiens (*Impatiens walleriana*) 10, 11, 41, 46, 120, 137, 143
Imperata cylindrica (*see* grasses—ornamental)
insecticide 68
invasive plants 8, 14, 66, 90, 95, 96, 127
Ipomoea purpurea (*see* morning glory)
iris 65
iris, bearded (*Iris germanica*) 128
islands 46, 47
Itea virginica (*see* Virginia sweetspire)
ivy 26, 31, 43, 45, 46, 81, 143
  as container plants 145

J
Jacob's ladder (*Polemonium*) 125
  variegated 126
Japanese beetle 69, 173
  control 69
Japanese painted fern (*Athyrium niponicum* 'Pictum') 126
Japanese spurge (*Pachysandra*) 15, 43, 63, 88, 91, 125
Japanese tree lilac (*Syringa reticulata* 'Ivory Silk') 115
Joe Pye weed (*Eupatorium maculatum*) 123
juniper (*Juniperus horizontalis*) 91

K
Katsura tree (*Cercidiphyllum japonicum*) 115
kiwi vine (*Actinidia kolomikta*) 111
Kniphofia (*see* red-hot poker)
Kolkwitzia amabilis (*see* beauty bush)

L
lacewings 66
lady's mantle (*Alchemilla mollis*) 122, 125
ladybugs 65
Lamiastrum galeobdolon (*see* yellow archangel)
Lamium (*see* dead nettle)
Lamium maculatum (*see* spotted dead nettle)
Lathyrus odoratus (*see* sweet pea)
Latin names 8
lawns
  feeding 87
  grubs 85
  maintenance 36, 84
  mowers 88
  mowing hillsides 86

reducing 39, 85
sprinklers—choosing 78, 87
trimming 86
watering 87
leaves: fall clean-up 171
lettuce 154
liatris (*Liatris spicata*) 122
Liatris (*see* blazing star)
licorice plant (*Helichrysum*) 145
Ligularia (*dentata*) 123
lilies (genus *Lillium*) 141
Lillium Longiflorum (*see* Easter lilies)
lily-of-the-valley (*Convallaria*) 43, 91, 125
littleleaf linden (*Tilia cordata*) 116
lobelia 145
Lonicera (*see* honeysuckle)
lungwort (*Pulmonaria longifolia*) 43, 131
lupin (*Lupinus* x *hybrida*) 65, 125, 129
Lychnis (*see* Maltese cross)

M
magnolia
   saucer (*Magnolia* x *soulangiana*) 117
   star (*Magnolia stellata*) 117
maidenhair tree (*Ginkgo biloba*) 115, 116
mallow (*Hibiscus*) 125, 165
Maltese cross (*Lychnis*) 125
manure 53, 58, 59, 74, 89, 125, 148, 154,
   155, 169, 173
maple
   amur (*Acer ginnala*) 115
   Japanese (*Acer palmatum* 'Bloodgood')
   115
marigolds 10, 11, 41, 65, 120
meadow-rue (*Thalictrum delavayi* 'Hewitt's
   Double') 126
meadowsweet (*Filipendula rubra* 'Venusta')
   124
microclimates 25
Miscanthus sinensis 'Morning Light' (*see* grasses
   —ornamental)
Miscanthus sinensis (*see* grasses—ornamental)
Molinia caerulea 'Variegata' (*see* grasses—
   ornamental)
monkshood (*Aconitum napellus*) 43, 125,
   131
morning glory (*Ipomoea purpurea*) 165
mother of thyme (*Thymus serpyllum*) 91
mugo pine (*Pinus mugo*) 113
mulch 29, 32, 33, 43, 45, 46, 56, 59, 60,
   63, 73, 85, 88, 89, 94, 111, 126, 142,
   149
   inorganic 60
Myosotis sylvatica (*see* forget-me-not)

N
nitrogen 61
Nootka false cypress (*Chamaecyparis
   nootkatensis* 'pendula') 113

O
obedient plant—variegated (*Physostegia
   virginiana* 'Variegata') 127
onions 154
ornamental (*Allium giganteum*) 127
organic matter. 51
oriental poppy (*Papaver orientale*) 125

P
Pachysandra (*see* Japanese spurge)
Paeonia (*see* peony)
Panicum virgatum (*see* grasses—ornamental)
pansies 10, 41, 120
Papaver orientale (*see* oriental poppy)
parsley 66, 145, 148, 155, 164, 165
parsnips 151
paths 28, 32, 46
patios 45
peas 154
peat moss 23, 24, 52, 53, 59, 89, 103, 125,
   142, 143, 161, 163, 165
Pelargonium (*see* geranium, annual)
Pennisetum alopecuroides (*see* fountain
   grass)
Pennisetum setaceum 'Rubrum' (*see* grasses—
   ornamental)
peony (*Paeonia*) 122, 125, 144
peppers 154
perennial beds 132
   maintenance 37
   dividing 124
perennials
   "Gentle Giants" 123
   "Kissing Cousins" 127
   "Prima Donnas" 128
   "Shady Ladies" 130
   "Trusted Old Friends" 121
   "Welcomed Strangers" 125
   fall care 133
   feeding and watering 133
   planting 133
pergolas 27, 110, 144
periwinkle (*Vinca major; V. minor*) 88, 91
perlite 143, 161, 163
Perovskia atriplicifolia (*see* Russian sage)
pesticides
   and insecticides 64
   as a last alternative 70
   organic over chemical 71
pests 64, 65
   slugs 131
petunias 11, 41, 139
   as container plants 145
phlox (*Phlox paniculata*) 65, 129
phosphate content 25
phosphorous 61
Physostegia virginiana (*see* obedient plant)
Picea abies (*see* bird's nest spruce)
Picea omorika (*see* Serbian spruce)

pincushion flower (*Scabiosa columbaria*
    'Butterfly Blue' or 'Pink Mist') 126
pine needles 56
pinks (*Dianthus*) 125
Pinus mugo (*see* mugo pine)
Pinus nigra (*see* Austrian pine)
planning for spring 82
plantain lily (*see* hosta)
plants
    as "heroes" 99
    choosing a site 7, 9
    easy-going and reliable 35
    in platoons 9
    "Fast Food" types 10
    labelling 81
    locations 23
    moving 24
    set beneath large trees 43
Polemonium (*see* Jacob's ladder)
Polygonum affine (*see* fleeceflower)
Polygonum aubertii (*see* silverlace vine)
Polygonatum multiflorum (*see* Solomon's seal)
primrose (*Primula*), 43, 132
propagation 159
    "Damping off" 162
    beginner selections 164
    choosing seeds 163
    cold frames 168
    containers 161
    handling small seeds 165
    hardening off 168
    light needs 166
    lighting 160
    scarification 165
    soil 161, 163
    stratification 165
    transplanting 167
pruning 108, 109, 118
    location on stem 75
    paint 31
    plastic sheet 82
    shrubs and small trees 31
Pulmonaria longifolia (*see* lungwort)
purple coneflower (*Echinacea purpurea*) 9, 123

R
rain barrels 79
red-hot poker (*Kniphofia*) 125
rhododendrons 22, 56, 102, 112, 142
Rodgersia pinnata 'Elegans' (*see* featherleaf
    rodgersia)
rose mallow (*Hibiscus*) 125, 129
rosemary 145, 148, 155
rose-of-Sharon (*Hibiscus syriacus*) 108
roses
    hybrid tea 37, 44, 65
    maintenance 44
    pests and diseases 9
    shrub roses 37, 44

Royal Botanical Gardens 13, 100
Rudbeckia fulgida (*see* black-eyed Susan)
Rudbeckia hirta (*see* gloriosa daisy)
Russian sage (*Perovskia atriplicifolia*) 127

S
sage (herb) 121, 123, 127, 148
sage, blue (*Salvia superba*) 121
salvia, blue (*Salvia farinacea*) 136
Salvia superba (*see* sage, blue)
Scaevola (*see* fan-flower)
Scabiosa columbaria (*see* pincushion flower)
Sedum (*see* stonecrop)
seed-heads as bird food 172
Serbian spruce (*Picea omorika*) 113
shade 7, 10, 11, 22, 26, 42, 43, 65, 86, 88,
    102
    types 42, 43
shade-loving plants 43
shrubs 23
    "creative pruning" 29
    favourite low-maintenance 104–108
    maintenance 37
    preparing site 103
    pruning 31, 108, 109
    selection and spacing 100–103
    transplanting from container 103
    trouble-shooting 109
Siberian pea-shrub (*Caragana arborescens*
    'Pendula') 106
silver sage (*Artemesia ludoviciana*) 11, 123
silverlace vine (*Polygonum aubertii*) 111
snapdragons (*Antirrhinum majus*) 41, 120,
    137
snow-in-summer (*Cerastium*) 125
soaker hoses 78
soil
    analysis 52
    assessing and modifying 50
    creatures 51
    preparation 51
    types 53
Solomon's seal (*Polygonatum multiflorum*)
    43, 132
sphagnum moss 163
spider flower (*Cleome spinosa*) 137
spiraea
    bridalwreath (*Spiraea prunifolia*) 7
    dwarf (*Spiraea x bumolda*) 85, 107
spotted dead nettle (*Lamium maculatum*)
    91
spring bulbs
    choosing and planting 140
    maintenance 37
spurge (*Euphorbia*) 125, 127
squash 154
St. John's wort (*Hypericum prolificum*) 93,
    106
statuary 27

stonecrop
  (*Sedum*) 11
    dragon's blood (*Sedum spurium*) 92
    goldmoss (*Sedum acre*) 92
    showy (*Sedum spectabile* 'Autumn Joy') 123
straw 56
summer bulbs 36
summersweet clethra (*Clethra alnifolia*) 106
sweet pea (*Lathyrus odoratus*) 165
sweet William (*Dianthus barbatus*) 139
sweet woodruff (*Galium odoratum*) 89, 92
Syringa reticulata (*see* Japanese tree lilac)

T
tansy (*Chrysanthemum vulgare*) 68
Thalictrum delavayi (*see* meadow-rue)
thyme 91, 145, 148, 155
Thymus serpyllum (*see* mother of thyme)
tickseed (*Coreopsis verticillata* 'Moonbeam')
  123
Tilia cordata (*see* little leaf linden)
toads 67
tomato cages 80
tomatoes 151
tools
  choosing quality 73
  cultivators 74
  handles 74
  lopping shears 77
  power 73
  pruners 75
  pruning saws 77
  shears and saws 74
  spades and forks 73
  trowels 74
transplant fertilizer 25, 61
trees
  "topping" 118
  choosing low-maintenance types 114–117
  pruning 118
turnip 156
turtlehead (*Chelone obliqua*) 132

V
vegetables 42, 57, 61, 147, 148, 153, 165,
  168
  choosing 151
  kitchen gardens 155
  minimizing maintenance 151
  rotating crops 149
  rows and beds 148
  scheduling harvest 149
vermiculite 143, 163
viburnum-doublefile (*Viburnum plicatum*
  var. tomentosum) 106
vinca (*Catharanthus rosea*) 137
Vinca major; V. minor (*see* periwinkle)
vines and ivy 110–111
Virginia sweetspire (*Itea virginica*) 106

W
water features 45
water gardens 46
watering cans 78
watering wands 78
weeds 63
  controlling without herbicides 64
  controlling with mulch 59
  prevention and control 62
wheelbarrows and carts 79
witchhazel, vernal (*Hamamelis vernalis*) 106
wood chips 57

Y
yellow archangel (*Lamiastrum galeobdolon*
  'Herman's Pride') 126
yews (*Taxus*) 113

Z
zinnias 65
zucchini 155